AT LEAST I'M WHITE
Untenable

AT LEAST I'M WHITE
Untenable

ORIS T. WINN JR.

Table of Contents

ACKNOWLEDGEMENT

A simple observation of the daily life experiences, on local, national, and global platforms, as seen though and by what some will refer to as a member of a Minority status, socially, spiritually, emotionally and culturally. Some will possibly label this as a biased undertaking. Be very careful of your assessments and judgements. Until you have walked a mile in my shoes, experienced the unacceptable, the denials, and battled beyond the visible walls of non-acceptance, non-beliefs, and non-inclusion, please allow me a moment to vent.

Inevitably some will view this book as yet another in the long line of those whining and complaining of life that exists within the U.S., and "what should be" manuscripts. Of that assertion there is truth, but to label this book as being written by someone who isn't proud to be American, and a Bitter Black American for that matter is something that is so contrary and distant from what is true. This is a book that will serve to merely, awaken and admonish some of the Truths of Differences that are alive and shamefully well within the U.S., to warn some who either ignorantly, arrogantly, and or passively deny such differences, and

1

educate us all of what is possible with the correction of monumental differences within a "divided" United States of America, that God has crowned thy good with Brotherhood, from Sea to Shining Sea.

Jesus, I'll never forget what you've done for me, what you're doing for me, and the ultimate sacrifice you made for me. Thank you, Jesus, for being the shining example of giving, and service. Thank you for the teaching and forewarning of the disappointments that are often felt within sacrifice. Yet, as the Apostle Paul stated, "I'm forgetting those things which are behind me, and I'm pressing toward the mark of the High calling in Jesus Christ"!

My Grandmother, Baby Ruth Winn, taught me very well that whenever anyone does something nice, something encouraging, something that brings about positive results, be very sure to if nothing else, say THANK YOU! My lists of THANK YOU in the composing and completion of this book is quite long and I'm sure some names will be left off in print, yet never in my heart of gratitude. Believe me, all who have encouraged, pushed, implored upon me, and told me, I could do this thing are appreciated more than mere words can say, or be written. First in my heart, mind, body, and soul, my Lord and Savior Jesus

2

Christ, who daily reminds me and whispers in my Spirit, Yea though you walk through the Valley and Shadow of Death, why are you fearing, I'm constantly with you, and you can do all things through Me, just keep stepping Jr.! Thank you, Lord, for the assignment, for the push, the courage, and for the patience, when my own was questionable. You always remind me that anything I may need on this journey, just as you reminded Moses in your Mighty Declaration, I AM! Thanks Bishop T.D. Jakes for reminding me and others that "I'M Almost there", Rev. Lester Love, for emphasizing, "I Can, I Will, I Must, Dr. Myles Munroe, for the teaching of Vision, Rev. Samuel Rodriguez for the sermon and teaching of the "CRUSHING" required for the extraction of the precious ointment within, Joseph Prince for the teaching of God's Unmerited Favor towards us all. To my Pastor, Rev. Roy F. Jones Jr., and his lovely wife, Sister Willie Mae Jones, who constantly remind me to keep on Pushing! My New Hope Missionary Baptist Church never cease praying for me and my family. To James and Tracie Garrett who have always had my back and encouraging words when I was in the Valley, to Anthony and Lorrie Sharpe who have always given a heartfelt push, to Charles and Nicole Miller for your

3

inspiration! I am so very blessed by you all. To the Song master, Carl Lee Milligan, who would always ask, "where's the book, Man!" To Arthur and Ruby Davis, you know! Leonard and Chesma McCoy continue to be the SHIFT needed in this world! James, David and Missy Houston, you guys touch my heart always.

God is truly blessing me through my family, my children, my grandchildren, and my great grandchild, Tamara, Tiffany, Oris Tyran, Detric, Tierra, Daijon, Oris Tyran Jr., Toure, and JaMya, my brothers(in-law) James and Johnny Jackson, Will Beadles, and Sam Thomas my sisters(in-law) Charlotte Jackson, Lelar Beadles, and Dorothy Thomas. Little Ty, you have always been my inspiration and joy, and then up pops JaMya, thank you Lord, all you guys, know that I Love you all very much, no matter what! To my sister, "Seeya" Ruth Etta Lake, you know that I Love and thank God for you, and your Baby Ruth tenacity.

Thank you, Mama, Baby Ruth, Mama Barbara, Daddy Oris Sr., who all constantly reminded me of the importance of Jesus, and thank you Mama Jo, for your sweet encouragement, patience, and Love.

I would be remised if I were to leave out the young man who unknowingly proved to be the biggest incentive, the stimulus if you will for the writing of this book. The young Caucasian, Travis Rebel Basketball player, so shook up, so frustrated about the downfall of his team that he resorted to the only thing he felt available that would hurt me mentally and spiritually, a forward attack and proclamation to remind me of my "place" in the social strata of the United States, yet that proclamation has served to lift and inspire me, when in his best red faced, chest thumping bravado, defiantly and proudly shouted "AT LEAST I'M WHITE'! The only word he left out, that I was sure was salivating, drooling, and dripping, and aching to come out was NIGGER. He meant it for my bad, BUT GOD is to this very second working it out for my GOOD. So sad, this young man, and so many like him today, could make such a statement relying completely upon the effect of which he has wrongly perceived, without properly addressing the causes of said effect!

To all of those knowingly and unknowingly, God has assigned to my Life, and this assignment, please accept my heartfelt, Thank You!

Now in the vernacular of the young'uns, "It's time to get to the purnt (point), let's get it poppin'! I'm at the point in my stage of my life chronologically that most of my years on this side are behind me, yet my best spirit filled, inspiration filled hope filled years are before me. God promised, my latter days will be greater than my former days, and I'm holding HIM to HIS Promise. Believe me, I realize that to get some to read this book and think, to understand this book, will be as likely as selling chains to slaves, and rain to fire, yet with God's Guidance, I will persevere.

Thank you, Rev. Samuel Rodriguez for your admonishing and reminder that, it's time to move, and to act quickly", the night isn't upon us yet, but the shadows are looming large, and that there exists a thin line between pathetic, and prophetic.

Billy Preston sang a song that contained the lyrics, "will it go round in circles, or will it fly high like a bird up in the sky?" It is past time for the breaking of unfruitful cycles! When we can change our minds, we can change our world, when we can change our attitude, we'll change our altitude, and when we can educate, we will surely elevate. We must get out of these cycles that hold our nation, and our people in grips of perpetual negativity.

My people perish for a lack of knowledge--Hosea 4:6

As a rainbow coalition of people, we must all come to the realization that, we are all, chosen to be challenged, challenged to be blessed, and blessed to be chosen.

All things work toward the good....
Romans 8:28

There is a way that seems right unto man, yet the end thereof leads to destruction...
Proverbs 16:25

Beware of any quick fix, get rich schemes and solutions that are at the expense of any segment of society, justified by calling and deeming that segment, "Social, collateral damage.

Enter ye in at the strait gate, for wide is the way that leadeth to destruction, and many there be which go in there at....Matthew 7:13

Must it be necessary that evil snarls its hideous face, before "True Love" is manifested and activated?

For wherever Christ builds a Church, the devil builds

7

a Temple----Martin Luther

I can only imagine if we were to all Love Now.

NOW-*Now faith is the substance--Heb. 11:1*

IF-*If my people which are called by my name 2 Chron. 7:14*

YE- *Ye are the salt of the earth--Matt: 5:13*

LET-*Let this mind be in ye--Phil. 2:5*

LOVE-*Love ye, one another--John 15:12*

My brothers and sisters, I truly pray for that day when the United States of America, truly becomes one Nation, Indivisible, under ONE GOD. A nation where all are granted the opportunity to attain their "AT MOST'S" far removed from the excuses of the "AT LEAST'S"!

Some will ask, what is the answer, what is the solution.

MANY DIFFERENCES yet in need of ONE LOVE!

Think about this; there is a big difference between All One, and Alone. As it is with this nation, if true unity isn't found within All of our Hearts, and any one segment is ignored, and denied, AL(L) ONE, will find itself A(L)ONE in a nation that is supposedly built on the platform of Liberty and Justice for ALL!

INTRODUCTION

I have been contemplating, debating, wrestling, and wondering on the necessity of writing this book in particular because of the subject matter it will entail. I realize some will say that I have a slanted view of the subject matter, and in my opinion that side hopefully will be viewed as that of justice, spirituality, and equality. I also realize that in many ways I will also be, as John the Baptist believed, "A voice crying in the Wilderness", a voice for that of righteousness.

I have for the past three years, pondered what would be the use of such an endeavor, yet this project just won't leave me alone. Subject matter pertaining to the book is produced and crops up hourly, and daily, even in this the twenty first century. Whether there be only one or a million that will read this book, I am saying something I am compelled to think and say quite honestly on a daily basis. I also realize that to some the writing of a book, particularly on Race Relations within the United States of America, would be especially by those within the Status Quo considered a massive mundane and unnecessary chore of stirring up muddy water, or even a labor if you will, but I have grown enough in my moral and spiritual walk to realize that a job is quite different than that of work. For as stated in the Bible, I must work the work of Him that sent me, while it is day, for the night comes that no man can work. It is not quite sundown yet, but the shadows loom larger.

Please bear with me as I meditate, review, then express some of the episodes in the daily life, and life experiences along racial boundaries which I hope will make this book not only interesting and thought provoking but also a necessary instrument that will compel the reader whether black, white, brown, red, or yellow to do some serious self-examination, and honest soul searching, and hopefully come to some repentance.

If this is truly the Land of the Free, and the Home of the Brave, Indivisible with liberty and Justice for All, there would be absolutely no need what so ever for the thoughts, and emotions that have been pushed forward, and will be examined in this Book. If we don't face our demons, they will as they have since this nation's inception most assuredly fester, as an all-consuming malignant cancer, and continue to haunt, perplex, twist, and gnaw on our very intellectual, moral, and spiritual fiber. If our demons aren't successfully confronted, we will not only continue our rapid descent into hell in a hand basket, we will be going on a downward well-greased spiral, in gasoline drenched underwear, that no legion of firefighters will be able to contain, let alone extinguish.

If we can change our minds, we can change our world, if we can change our attitude, we can change our altitude, if we can educate, we can and will most assuredly elevate. We are not by no means whatsoever perfect, but we must make progress toward escaping the miry clay of complacency, and thick mud of negativity, and venture closer to aforementioned aspirations, "That day when all of God's Children......realize, truly we are all God's children.

I also love the Television Commercial on race relations that states "Imagine the power of one voice" a powerful and crystal -clear statement.

Well ladies and gentlemen, boys and girls, black and white, the moment has arrived for my voice to be heard! So, let us examine the Social, Economic, and Political landscape of this the United States of America! One Nation that should be UNDER GOD.

UNTENABLE

UN TEN A BLE - (adj.)-(especially of a position or view) not able to be maintained or defended against .attack or objection

UNTENABLE, a seldom used four syllable word within the English Language that society demands should be included and examined. Its origin undoubtedly originated from actions, attitudes, and agendas that have existed far past what should have been their expiration date.

To believe the attitude and profess such attitudes as to insinuate ones supposed Superiority over another either boldly or covertly is UNTENABLE. To express one's racial pride to the inclusion of One Nation under God, with Liberty and Justice for all should be self-explanatory as compared to Racial Pride EXCLUSIVE of those contrary to one's thoughts and skin tone. Ones who speak of Purity of Race without regard to Purity of Creation and Mankind, UNTENABLE.

A Child is born with a heart of Gold, ways of the world make that Heart so cold-EARTH, WIND, & FIRE.

Everything begins with a Thought, if said thoughts

13

of negativity are paramount, UNTENABLE nature festers.

After examining and exposing various episodes in my life, I pray this book will be read and examined as a manuscript that is attempting to expose, and cause thoughts and actions to remedy, and cause some possible repentance, and resolution to the scourge that is UNTENABLE. Excuse me if the book may seem to skip from various time frames, yet I pray that a readable flow has been achieved. Be Patient with me, God is not finished with me. As an Author, and a Man, I am a work in Progress.

The thoughts presented in AT LEAST I'M WHITE, UNTENABLE, are thoughts on past, and current situations, attitudes, and actions that should not have ever occurred within the Souls of Men and the Soul of a Nation, whose foundation is based on and established as One Nation, Under God, Indivisible, with Liberty and Justice for ALL Of those thoughts, some will counter in their defense, "what happened back then is over, and THEY should get over it", and I will counter, what happened back then, is happening NOW, the only difference is it has chosen a new DANCE PARTNER, a new agenda, a new strategy.

14

This book is my personal account of a few of my journeys and thoughts as I have navigated through an "AT LEAST I'M WHITE" WORLD. Whether you enjoy the material within is not my mission, my mission is to prod, and instigate thought that has been stagnant in some's comfort zone, and hopefully encourage change where change need be. Be Blessed in a Nation whose Pretense is that of Love of Nation, to the exclusion of any segment of its society.

INOPPORTUNITY-UNTENABLE
NON-EXPOSURE-UNTENABLE
EXCLUSIVE SOCIETY-UNTENABLE
TUNNEL VISION-UNTENABLE
RACIAL INEQUALITY-UNTENABLE
CRIMINAL, CRIMINALJUSTICESYSTEM -UNTENABLE
I'VE GOT MINE, TO HELL WITH YOURS-UNTENABLE

Some who would think that just because of the pigmentation of their Skin qualifies them to possess all the qualities necessary to be better than me- UNTENABLE
Without further ado, ladies and gentlemen, I Present for your reading pleasure or displeasure, "AT LEAST I'M WHITE, UNTENABLE.

15

Chapter 1

Nobody Told Me, In the Beginning

Nobody told me that the road would be easy, but I don't believe He's brought me this far to leave me! In writing this book I realize I will have many nay-sayers, and those who will fail to recognize themselves in the passages. I will be questioned, and I will have haters. I will question and endure spiritual debates. Nevertheless, this book is an assignment that continues to be what purpose demands of me. No matter how mundane, needless, and or controversial anyone may feel this book to be, it continues to demand of me to be, and I hold no grudges if you are to stop its reading, I understand these things will occur. If this is to happen to you, please examine the reasons provoking your action! Is it guilt, and unwillingness to examine one's self, or is it the arrogancy to feel, "at least" I'm me, and no one is more qualified than myself, the real me, to call me into question. US the U.S., needs to collectively examine US, the U.S., bridge the divides, crown thy good, with brotherhood, from sea to shining sea!

16

"Each one has to find peace from within. And peace to be real must be unaffected by outside circumstances".
M. Gandhi

God has shed His Grace on Thee, yet it is difficult to imagine His satisfaction for what we've given in return; Our collective, At Least! Are we as a nation really walking, talking, and above all Loving as He has prescribed in His Holy Word? While the nation remains in the grips of division, it only stands to reason, much Favor is being delayed if not completely denied. Why is it, hate, bigotry and negativity increase at a supersonic pace, yet diminishes at the excruciating pace of a pre-global warming Glacial Iceberg?

It is surprising to me that some are yet to realize that the isometric exercises consisting soullessly of your judgement, (meant to diminish my self-esteem), and punishment(meant to hold me down in a cycle of denials) has only served to strengthen my determination in the pursuit of what should justly be mine. Don't believe me if you want, but I suggest you check with Samson, whose story is of biblical proportions, literally as well as figuratively. Through your arrogance, and turning your backs on your own, you have in essence led those denied to the Pillars of society and this government! You have gouged our eyes in an attempt to blind us, yet our VISION remains. Your hate is so much so, that unknowingly you have been blinded to the structures and monuments of bigotry, and hatred. Yet you seemingly can't see that your misguided values are slowly but most assuredly beginning to crumble.

The few, the proud, the elite! So sad, the few have the means to do the most yet pitifully are satisfied with doing the least in the arena of social assistance, edification, and change. Yet, they do the most in keeping what is theirs, in a closed fist, exclusive fraternal order.

Ain't it always the ones closest to the track, that seem to be the furthest from the race--Miller HiLife Commercial

Power in defense of freedom is greater that power in behalf of tyranny and oppression

Capital as such is not evil, it is its wrong use that is evil. Capital in some form or other will always be needed--M. Gandhi

The moment has arrived, it is now my turn at bat, my season to allow my voice to be heard, and for my words and thoughts to be conveyed! What I have to say will be pertinent to some, and to some irrelevant! Yet, these thoughts remain persistent within my psyche, so much so that I must give birth to that which is kicking within my soul! I must push out that which is within, to in some small way, possibly bring about the true Brotherhood of Mankind within this nation, the United States of America. Now is the time for us all to get up off our collective, complacent asses, in order to at least provide some positive, introspect, that will affect changes that will prove beneficial to current and future generations, black, white, brown, and yellow.

This will be a book that looks at a few of the components involved in the discourse, and desolation currently going on within this nation. Those components mainly being those of Greed, Selfishness, and Blatant and Covert Racism, which ironically some refer to as Racial Pride, where the sides are unequally yoked in unfair debate, and fights dealing with pertinent and relevant issues that deal with life, liberty, and the pursuit of Happiness!

Let's examine a few episodes in my life's history shall we. At the tender impressionable age of six years old, while on a weekend trip to Galveston Texas to **view** the Ocean and Beach for the first time, I also unknowingly experienced racial discrimination in the first of a long list of sad deplorable instances. This prominent episode stands out because it involves me, a six-year-old boy, who simply after a road trip from Houston had to pee! After continually being denied the use of Gas Station facilities, and in my innocence and urgency couldn't understand why the denial! My Daddy finally explained to me that Colored People weren't always granted the same privileges as White People, and that we would have to find a place where we would be accepted, and that sadly included certain areas of the Beach. Funny the waves came in for the whites just as well as they did for the blacks! MY Question then as a six-year-old, and as it is now is, Daddy Why? Please keep in mind that this happened in the fifties of the twentieth century.

While attending a newly integrated, "experimental" Junior High School, University Junior High, of Austin Texas, I encountered more conservative, good "ol" boy prejudice, than I would encounter liberal, caring white teachers and administrators. I endured, and triumphed

20

over tactics, statements, and actions that whether purposely or ignorantly administered were intended to derail and wreck me. Such statements as "all niggers have big lips and are stupid (this statement so crazy with the advent of tanning booths and Botox)! "I need you to go find that Nigger Boy" a command given to me by a teacher! To top things off I even had a Math teacher who divided and charted her class labeled Go Getters, and Ditch Diggers. Guess which group made for the biggest composition of Ditch Diggers! That teacher never caring what she was doing to the self-esteem of those students involved!

I bet you didn't have to guess too many times which group of students dominated the Ditch Digger genre and which group seemed to get more positive attention and individualized assistance.

I thank God for the Ruth Parker's (Science Teacher) who peaked my inquisitive mind, the Marsha Pitts (Speech and Drama instructor) who helped develop my oratory skills, the Lillian Browns,(English Literature instructor) who taught and furthered my literary skills, and the Toby Byrds (counselor) who exposed without prejudice, many young impressionable black minds and souls to the good, God given persona of the other

21

white side, those that viewed the world in shades of compassion.

During the late sixties, and early seventies, my High School years proved to be with little exception, the same segregation within the court ordered implementation of integration. The same preferential treatment of the supposed elite, the same, I'm teaching you because I have to, and not because I want to, totally devoid of passion and desire. The same, I'm better than you, uncaring stares, the same snide remarks prerequisite for those attending a High School named after a High School named after a Civil War Confederate Librarian, John H. Reagan, and whose Principal was named Jefferson Davis Hill! These things seemed to be more than coincidence especially when the Principal would sometimes literally weep during recitation of the Pledge of Allegiance! Oh, and let me not fail to mention the proud display prominent within this principal's office of the United States Flag, Old Glory, The Texas State Flag, and 01' Dixie, the stars and bars of the Confederate States, apparently void, and uncaring of the dismay felt by those who knew what that flag represented.

I'd love to give a shout out to the teacher(?) who labeled me as a future Ditch-Digger, and later to her

22

dismay presided over my induction into the National Junior Honor Society. She never said a word, but her disappointment was written all over her face. God bless her, for God used her as a stepping stone, a catalyst, a springboard to a brighter future. Did she not know that Haters are the best elevators, and that opposition often gives birth to opportunity?

All things work toward the Good of those that Trust and Believe in the Lord and are called according to HIS PURPOSE--Romans 8:28

Now back to my friend who shouted, AT LEAST I'M WHITE, to which my response was with a chuckle, yeah man, shoot your best shot! He had just blurted out that to his thinking(?), he didn't have to be at his best on the basketball court or the court of life to be better than, or to best me, or to have a leg up on me in life, period! Well Duh! How silly of me to think differently? It remains sad to think that following and present generations, descendants of the founding fathers and slave owners to this day maintain that same train of thought. The thinking within that small rhetoric, AT LEAST I'M WHITE, is actually the musket ball within the muskets upon which this nation was established and stands.

23

This book is an attempt at the uncovering of the differences, and divisions, that are eroding the core values upon which this nation it built. I am writing this book in defense of those who are not being viewed, judged, and assessed fairly on supposed equal scales, as those of their counterparts. For those who are not given the same chances, opportunities, and love that should be paramount in the land of Liberty and Justice for all.

Some will ask, what is the solution, what is the cure for the ills of the Nation? To which I will reply, "It is Simple"! As with any disease of epic proportions, there will exist no semblance of a cure, until the symptoms are properly diagnosed, addressed, and hopefully successfully medicated, and eradicated. The problems within the racial interactions of this nation seemingly can be attributed to either an overabundance, or general lack thereof of four major factors, i.e., EDUCATION, EDIFICATION, ECONOMICS, and EGOS. Although we view life through different eyes, and from different cultural viewpoints, our common denominator that is striving to unite us, remains that of GENUINE LOVE of GOD and MANKIND. Please, we must conclude sooner, rather than later of the fact that, I need you, you need me, we're all a part of God's body! It is His will that every need be supplied, you are important to me, I need you to survive! A beautiful refrain from a lovely song celebrating unity. Let's just face it, WE ARE ONE. DIFFERENCES shouldn't be meant as means to divide, rather differences should be celebrated, examined, and used toward the elation of diversity, and the God given ability to act as the various, spices of life. One's gifts that are unique to that one, should not be celebrated any more than those of others . Rather, we are all various pieces of a Life puzzle that fit in perfectly to create a lovely landscape! How can I help you, how can you help me to get to the destination, God desires that WE all to reach?

Chapter 2
Mission Control

Mission Control to the Citizens of the United States of America, we have a PROBLEM with the Dream, and I Have a Dream. Key Problem being the Dream's Dual Perception. One being possessed by those who has already realized the DREAM, and the other is of he who is still trying to grasp the reins of the DREAM.

DREAM - (n) a series of thoughts, images, and sensations occurring in a person's mind during sleep

DREAM - (v) contemplate the possibility of doing something or that something might be the case.

NIGHTMARE - (n) a frightening or unpleasant dream a terrifying or very unpleasant experience or prospect. a person, thing, or situation that is very difficult to deal with. What happens when a Dream and Nightmare share Dual Citizenship, and there is no common ground to be found?

For far too long the Original Founding Forefathers and ancestors of those forefathers of this Nation, and those who feel that the Constitution and Bill of Rights were exclusively written to and for the benefit of THEIR exclusive sect, and to their dismay their DREAM for some seems to be unraveling, and it would appear that they feel that THEIR DREAM is too quickly becoming the Nightmare on Main Street, hence the slogans heard too often; We're taking our Country Back, Come and Take It, etc.! Their Bravado is nothing more than fear camouflaged as anger. Why would some for centuries do everything in their power to deny the American Dream for many, just to continue to hold the reins of the Democracy they have so proudly proclaimed? Then It occurred to me that they didn't mind when other sectors merely proclaimed to have a DREAM, just as long as said DREAM never has the opportunity of fruition. Their hope was that those who have been denied, and simply dream was that for that segment to, Sleep on my brother, sleep on.

There exists a problem with the DREAM! Foremost is the fear of the DREAM'S inevitable Fruition of Promise, and secondly, the possibility of those only satisfied with, and those who pray for the DREAM'S perpetual status of simply being a DREAM . Nothing comes to sleepers but a dream, was once sang by R&B artist Tevin Campbell, stating you can dream as long

27

as you want to, but the World still goes around and around. There would be monumental problems for the so-called status quo, if those satisfied with merely a DREAM would WAKE UP to the reality of God's Promises to ALL HIS CHILDREN! Does the possible reality of a DREAM fulfilled give birth to the nightmare of fear manifested through anger! How dare they allow their DREAMS to reach FRUITION! Could it be, that they have an AUDACITY OF HOPE?

In the current U.S. Government's installment of its forty fourth President's Administration of Congress and Senate, I cannot figure out for the life of me, how can a governing body's DREAM be based on the insurance of the Nightmare of probable failure of said government at the expense of the People of the Nation. Never mind what is good for the whole, as long as one's DREAM of total dominance is attained by any means necessary. Yet through the NIGHTMARE, one's DREAM like a Phoenix still arises.

For Seven years one's DREAM has been for the failure of the entire Nation. They have dreamt of the economy's failure, the rise of unemployment, the failure of our Healthcare System, and even terrorist attacks to guarantee the NIGHTMARE of the

President of their non-approval. Why would anyone pray the failure of one at the expense of an entire nation? DREAM or NIGHTMARE, it is of your choosing! NATION we have a problem with the DREAM, and its individual's interpretation of said DREAM.

Ones REALITY of LIFE, LIBERTY, AND THE PURSUIT OF HAPPINESS continues to be another's DREAM. There remains a PROBLEM with the DREAM!

For far too long, Black and White have grungily settled for an, AS IS status. We must all focus beyond the Cross of Inequality, and lawlessness to reach the Promised Land of Tranquility known as UNITED REALITY, far beyond DIVIDED DREAMS. There is nothing wrong with having high aspirations, and possessing a DREAM, the problem is to only possess the aspirations and dreams and to do little or nothing or not be allowed to have the opportunity to make those DREAMS and aspirations a reality!

Hebrews 12:2-Looking unto Jesus, the author and finisher of our faith, who for the joy that was set before Him endured the cross, despising the shame, and has sat down at the right hand of the throne of God.

I thank God for my ancestors, those who picked

29

cotton, those who on hands and knees mopped other people's floors, stood on bus stops through all types of weather, to go to the other side of town, who endured their crosses with a song and prayer and yes a DREAM that things would eventually be better for their children and grandchildren. Praying that their children would be able to stand on their feet, and not continually be bent, and having to live on their knees! The time for Dreaming is quickly drawing too slowly to a rolling halt. The time to WAKE UP is NOW quickly!

Hebrews 11:1-NOW FAITH is the substance of Things Hoped for, the evidence of things not seen.

Equality, not seen, Justice rarely seen, unison not seen, brotherhood of mankind rarely seen! It is past time for the DREAM to become reality through Faith, NOW! The "I HAVE A DREAM" speech by Martin Luther King Jr., was delivered over Fifty Years Ago, and people we are still chanting, "Keep the Dream Alive" and that is exactly what those opposed to the DREAM are depending on, that we Continue to Simply slumber as the DREAM is continually denied. A withered hand within a withered nation cannot

30

possibly move past a DREAM that some fear manifestation, unless we in unison STRETCH FORTH! So, I'm imploring upon us as a whole as a Nation, to WAKE UP! Just as Christ asked the man at the Pool of Bethesda who undoubtedly DREAMED of being healed, I am asking this Nation, WILST THOU BE MADE WHOLE?

The American Dream, a chicken in every pot, a nice home with a picket fence, a good job to provide for the family, opportunity to thrive freely without fear of retribution. A Reality for some, A Dream for far too many. The reality of inequality, injustice, and blatant differences simply because of SKIN Color must cease, prayerfully sooner rather than later. When will ALL, have a DREAM with a possibility of REALITY! Of FRUITION?

MISSION CONTROL OF THE UNITED STATES OF AMERICA, REALITY HAS LANDED, AND WE HAVE A PROBLEM WITH "THE DREAM"! WAKE UP! The Dream has served as a PACIFIER for far too long, it's time for the meat of the Promise!

Where Delusion and Dysfunction reigns, the harmony of Peace and the realization of Dreams will not and cannot exist, for the God of this Nation IS NOT the and will never be the author of Confusion. A

31

nation with a Dream, must be a nation void of Delusion, a nation with a Dream to be fulfilled must be void of Dysfunction!

Matthew 6:33 states the formula for the sum total of our Dreams; Seek YE(all of us) First, the Kingdom of God and His Righteousness, and all these things(Dreams Fulfilled) shall(will) be added unto you!

No one's true Dreams will ever be fulfilled where one's boot is standing upon the throat of those felt to be unworthy of the Promise the one with the boot is perceived to already possess. In order for the DREAM to reach its true Fruition, we must realize that, I need you, you need me, and we're all a part of God's Body! Please read 1Thes. 5:22-24 and realize as D. L. HUGHLEY often says in some of his comedy skits, we as a nation, NEED JESUS! When we change our delusional and dysfunctional Minds, we will change our World(Nation), when we change our negative attitudes, we will change our altitude, and when we EDUCATE, we will ELEVATE to where we as a Nation should BE!

THERE'S A PROBLEM WITH THE DREAM, THAT WILL NEVER BE RECTIFIED UNTIL WE

AS A NATION, WAKE UP!" We will never be ONE Nation, Under God, with Liberty, and Justice for All, if we insist on blocking DREAMS of some under the moniker of "AT LEAST"!

It is true, as the R&B Group of the '70's The Chilites sang, there will never be any Peace, (and Dreams Fulfilled) until God is at the Conference Table. For Dreams, For Life, For Truths Fruition, WE NEED JESUS to solve the Problems of the DREAM!

Abstain from all appearances of evil. And the very God of peace sanctify you wholly; and I pray God your whole spirit and soul and body be preserved blameless unto the coming of our Lord Jesus Christ. Faithful is he that calleth you, and also will do it.
1 Thes. 5:22-24

Chapter 3
It Was Good That I Was Afflicted

It was good that I was Afflicted, it led to my Promotion!

It is good for me that I have been afflicted. Even though the affliction came from bad men, it was overruled for good ends.--Psalms 119:71

But as for you, you meant evil against me, but God meant it for good, in order to bring it about as it is this day, to save many people alive.--Genesis 50:20

You thought that you had killed me, and buried me, only to realize that you had inadvertently planted me. Just as self-doubt had seemed to be at the point within me of raising its bloody fists and declaring victory, behind its banner of triumph, the recent tragic events along moral, ethical, and racial lines of indignation, shouted throughout my spirit, loudly, "Not so fast my Brother" you've received your command and commission, now finish the task at hand!

I cannot and will not conclude this book without addressing the paramount issue of Blatant, Ignorant, Entitled, Elitist Police Brutality, its unequal and unfair distribution of injustice, and apparent self-imposed righteousness, and legalization. The incidents in Chicago, Cleveland, Charleston, South Carolina, Waller County Texas, and McKinney Texas to name a "few", are screaming out in the lyrics of Marvin Gaye's 70's song and inquisition,

WHAT'S GOING ON?

MOTHER, MOTHER, THERE'S TOO MANY OF YOU CRYING

BROTHER, BROTHER, BROTHER, THERE'S FAR TOO MANY OF YOU DYING

YOU KNOW WE'VE GOT TO FIND A WAY, TO BRING SOME LOVIN' HERE TODAY

PICKET LINES, AND PICKET SIGNS, DON'T PUNISH ME WITH BRUTALITY

TALK TO ME, SO YOU CAN SEE, OH, WHAT'S GOING ON!

Just as I had come to the conclusion of thinking, what's the use, and had given into the stigma, commonly known as writer's block, and lastly resolved to defeat at the hands of that diabolical negative spirit known as Procrastination, up pops the various factions of the United States Gestapo Regime in many areas and instances, formerly known as Peace, and or Police Officers. Understand me please, I am not stating that all Officers are corrupt, yet, lately, there have been more than enough instances to cause one to go WHOA! WHAT'S REALLY GOING ON!? GESTAPO - Domain category act of terrorism, terrorist act (the calculated use of violence or threat of violence) against CIVILIANS in order to attain goals that are political or religious or ideological in nature; this is done through intimidation or coercion or instilling fear! Sound Familiar?

We've all heard the phrase, "One bad apple, doesn't spoil the whole bushel, yet in the cases of these mounting numbers of (BAD APPLES) GESTAPO UNITS, it gives one pause to consider, are there any good apples within a rotten bushel?

The "good/bad cop question can be disposed of decisively. We need only consider the following:

1. Every cop has agreed, as part of his job, is to enforce laws; all of them.

2. Many of the laws are manifestly unjust, or even cruel and wicked.

3. Therefore, every cop has agreed to act as an enforcer of laws that are manifestly unjust, or even cruel and wicked.

There are no good cops---Dr. Robert Higgs

How do I, why must I find it imperative, will I be able to adequately convey unto my children, grandchildren, and great-grandchildren, that, National Internal Terrorism is prevalent within the United States, and to be very cautious, and wary, for in more instances than not because of societal, and cultural differences, they will possibly overwhelmingly be the subjects of said TERRORISM, i.e., excessive (brutal) policing at the hands of rogue cops, as witnessed in episodes in Ferguson, Missouri, disgusting, New Jersey, disgusting, New York city, disgusting, Austin, Texas, disgusting, Chicago, disgusting, and the list seems to grow on a daily basis. DISGUSTING displays of man's inhumanity to(ward) man, at the hands of a few officers sworn to Protect, Serve, and Keep the Peace. "The Law" (Institutional

37

Racism) applied and subsequent punishment for breaking said laws is shamefully, blatantly and glaringly disproportionately distributed along racial lines within this nation of Liberty, and Justice for (all)! Some will suggest, that, surely, I exaggerate, yet facts seldom lie, and as the whole world watches, the truth remains that to be Black within the United States, whether guilty or innocent, you will in some way, every day, be a victim of governmental, and or societal sanctioned racism, and or terrorism ON A DAILY BASIS!

Despite differences displayed, I am determined to teach my children and grandchildren the importance of self-worth, great self-esteem, and love of and for your fellow man, and most importantly the blessings found within HUMILITY!

I am by no stretch of the imagination racist, nor a bigot, although I must admit that I am anti-ignorance. I am a staunch believer that not all white men are good, just as equally as I believe not all Black men are bad. Now more than any other time in this nation's history are Black Men being held to a higher standard especially in the arena of equal and fair treatment distributed by the Law, and subsequent consequences when one runs awry of said laws, whether proven guilty or innocent. So, with that being said, I am very concerned and troubled for my children, and grandchildren, who at any moment CAN be charged, judged, and executed at the hands of what has become the way too common ROGUE COP, using the ROGUE COP excuses; I feared for my life, THEY were resisting arrest, THEY had a weapon, THEY were going for my weapon, I mistook my taser for my gun, etc., etc., etc., lame excuses to follow through on JUSTIFIABLE(?) HOMICIDE.

What was it that the braggadocios young boy who over forty years ago know that he felt I wasn't aware of ? Was it from a place of pride or pity that he was aware that he wouldn't have to deal with the issues of life that I, and others as myself would be subjected to in this Nation! "AT LEAST I'M WHITE" a haunting declaration of entitlement, a statement that sadly describes the sentiment felt by far too many upstanding citizens of this nation.

Oh, but to be a nation of neutrality, a nation that is color blind rather than color centered, Oh, just to be a God-centered man, void of world-imposed stigmas!

A. North Charleston, S.C.-gunned down like a dog, shot eight times in the back, while being video-taped unaware--HE went for my gun!!

B. Choked out by one cop, as three other cops look on as the unarmed suspect repeats, and pleas continually, "I CAN'T BREATHE"!

C. A police dog is allowed to maul a handcuffed unresponsive suspect who later dies in the streets of New Jersey--I feared for my life!

D. An Arizona College Professor brutally accosted by Campus Security for failing to provide proper campus identification--I feared I'd get a paper cut(?)

E. To be fatally shot in the back of the neck, during a foot chase in Austin, Texas--MY weapon, accidentally discharged at the base of suspects neck.

F. Fatally shot in Tulsa, Oklahoma by a volunteer Police Benefactor who mistook his Revolver for his taser--inexcusable!

Pitifully the list of outrageous examples of Police Department abuses of power and excessive force, particularly against people of color grows at what seem to be warp speed daily! The common denominator of these list is that of overzealous, over protected, above the Law White Rogue Cops with little fear of repercussions, and in many cases commentated for their actions in the performing of their "duties". I've heard the adage about keeping your friends close, and your enemies closer, yet in the case of the BAD COP, their perceived enemy is executed before being allowed to plead their case.

My Grandson once asked me, "why do they hate us because of the color of our skin"? I brokenheartedly had to explain that HATE is a strong word and even stronger emotion, closely tied to FEAR. Fear of possible loss, i.e.," we're taking our country back", plus disdain, backed by ignorance, GUNS, tasers, and corrupt justice systems. Justice Systems in the hands of cowards equate to, if we are Lucky to live, a stint in Prison, and the continued disjointing of our strongest unit; The Family, and if unlucky we end up with results similar if not worse than South Carolina, New York, Muskogee and Tulsa Oklahoma, , Ferguson

Missouri, Bastrop and Austin Texas, Waller County Texas, and shamefully the list goes on and on.

Obsessed with power void of compassion, and an overwhelming fear of possibly losing its grip on said power has led to the scary foreboding, and conclusion for some of the possibility of as Malcom X once stated, The Chickens are coming home to roost! These thoughts quite possibly have led to FEAR camouflaged as HATE from the sense of possible depletion. Could it all be slipping away?!

INCOMPREHENSIBLE - Not able to understand, not intelligible

DESPICABLE - Deserving hatred and contempt

LUDICROUS - Causing laughter because of absurdity

DASTARDLY - Wicked and cruel, cowardly; characterized by underhandedness or treachery, despicable, diabolical, heinous

Just as some of other ilk's view those of my particular ilk as the trashy discarded USED gum, stuck

42

on the soles(souls) of their shoes(being). Could it also be, that due to your stiff necked, hard hearted views, you are seen by many as the oily, nasty, elixir that has been spilt and has left a nasty stain on the fabric of the American Tapestry. So far that stain, even the strongest detergent has thus far been unable to remove. The stain of hate, and guilt has thus far been able to hide from the intensified, industrialized TIDE of change!

When evil deeds and words are being tolerated in a civil society, that indifference is in and of itself evil. Thank you, Dr. Cornell West for reminding me of the Sly and the Family Stones hit, R&B tune, STAND. the particular lyric that still hits home today is "There's a midget standing tall, and a Giant beside him about to fall, STAND"!

Yes, some are quick to claim the moniker and self-imposed privilege associated to the proclamation, AT LEAST I'M WHITE, and these are usually the very one to say or do the Least to bring about a true resolution for a nation of Liberty and Justice for ALL. The LEAST possessing the LEAST concern is of itself evil. Are we not our Brother's Keeper? I guess it is true, as the Miller High Life commercial suggested, that "Doesn't it always seem that the ones closest to the

43

Track, are usually the furthest away from the race"! The very ones who can do the MOST, are sadly the same ones who are willing to do the LEAST toward the HEALING OF THIS NATION'S ILLS.

To continually ignore and fail to indict criminal acts of human, social, and racial indignation has become the "Silence" of complacency indicative of Approval. What could have been prevented has now become a "Silence", that hopefully has given birth to a "Roar" for change. WAKE UP!!

The determination of the choice between Life or Death is not mine to decide. Although I may be the master of my fate, and captain of my soul, I am not nor never will purposely be the malicious taker of another's life, where humanly possible, and where other means to subdue possible perpetrators that endanger another's life is viable. My Lord and Savior is my vindicator as well as my witness. All power in Heaven and on Earth are under His Divine Rule.

As I conclude this book, sadly, on a daily basis my thoughts are turned to the ever-increasing lawlessness of this nation's various Law Enforcement Agencies, from sea to shining sea, and its unequal repugnant and far too often fatal distribution of "Dodge City" justice. But in Dodge City, it was considered cowardly to shoot another in the back! These are not only the Police of Reality Shows such as COPS and COPS RELOADED (RELOADED, RELOADED, REALLY, REALLY). I'm writing of the corrupt Cops who shout and fatally shoot, shouting all the while, stop resisting arrest, I feared for my life, I have a Revolver in my hand that I mistook for my taser, oops, my bad, the armed, mentally, and morally deprived dangerous cops.

It is pro-ponderous, that we are "living" in a time that, what is plainly seen with our own eyes, is clearly and legally in conflict with what we thought we saw. It all depends on WHOSE eyes and CONSCIOUS the TRUTH is seen through. The Judges for the most part is seemingly on Cruise Ships for profit, joining corrupt Prosecutors, Bail bondsmen, and CEO'S of Prisons for Profit Institutions, and guess who makes up the main commodity to keep these institutions profitable, and rows the boat that keep the Cruise Ship afloat. This is one of the ugliest displays of contentious, and despicable, Supply and Demand!

Some will undoubtedly be in a quandary, and some will certainly not give a damn as to the reasons and necessity of writing a book that shines a tiny light on the plight of racial discrimination, which deserves a thousand-watt spotlight, whether consciously or subconsciously upon the souls and minds of many, here, in the Twenty First Century, in what is becoming ever more evidently the DIVIDED (UNITED) States of America. When asked to validify my previous statement, one needs to look no further than;

A. WHITE ONLY Customers signs placed on various businesses located in the regentrified, once predominately Black neighborhoods of Austin Texas.

B. Proposed and recently passed legislation to allow open carry of handguns, even within classrooms in the state of Texas.(2015)

C. "Run Nigger, Run practice targets at gun ranges in South Dakota.(2015)

D. Sigma Alpha Epsilon Fraternity's chant of "Never be a Nigger SAE, at the University of Oklahoma(2015)

E. A young Black suspect while fleeing FROM the Police in Muskogee Oklahoma, is shot in the BACK, by an overweight out of shape Cop, who incidentally feared for his life as the suspect was running away from him as another Cop was approaching from the opposite direction.(2015)

These are only a few examples of why "AT LEAST I'M WHITE" is being written.

When Officer Blue Badge, evolves into protected from indictment Officer Blue Shield, depends upon the Blue Code of Silence, which in most instances guarantees "who you gonna call" exoneration. In far too many instances for minority citizens, these TOP (Thugs on Patrol) Cops have become more of the Ghost Makers than the Peace Keepers. How can Scum, rid the streets and neighborhood of perceived Scum!?

Chapter 4
The Lust of The Flesh, Lust of The Eye, and The Pride of Life

The LUST OF THE FLESH, LUST OF THE EYE, and the PRIDE OF LIFE, (I John 2:16)

This statement and its scriptural reference have pretty much accurately assessed the conditions that are prevalent within the United States today.

Dan 5:25--Mene, Mene, Tekel, Upharsin--which is to be interpreted as "your Kingdom has been examined and has been found to be wanting, and lacking, especially when it comes to God, His ways, His truth, and His Life!

GALL - Brazen boldness coupled w/impudent assurance and insolence

INSOLENCE--back talk, sass

INSOLENT--contemptuous in speech or conduct

CONTEMPTUOUS--manifesting feeling, or expressing deep hatred, or disapproval, feeling or showing contempt

GUMPTION--common sense-horse sense, courage and confidence

IMPUDENT--failing to show proper respect and courtesy.

What happens when the creation takes of the characteristics contrary to those of the creator? What happens when the creation takes on a me, myself, and I attitude toward life, and believes (it) is the ultimate within creation? (1 Cor: 14:33) - For God is not the author of confusion, but of peace, as in all churches of the saints.

Phil 4:13--I can do all things through Christ, who strengthens me; **love, overcome, persevere, achieve, and exemplify that which is of my Lord, and Savior Jesus** *Christ (Shouldn't this be the mindset of God's crowned jewel of creation?)*

The audacity of gumption to call out the audacity of gall. The undertaking of this Endeavour is to point out differences that to this day remain amongst all of mankind, particularly within the United States of America, in this day and time (?), the twenty first century. COME ON MAN! Some would question my raking around in the coals of human complacency, and interaction, especially racial interaction, when lukewarm seems to work fine for those existing especially on the high end of the stick, to the detriment of those existing on the lower end of the stick ((What happens when boy is perceived to have dominion over man?), as long as everything is STATUS QUO!, as long as I've got mine, and I could give a damn about you getting yours, especially if mine is thought to be better than yours.

Some will say, why are you rocking the boat of neutrality, at least you are able to go to school with US, you are allowed to vote with us, you can dine with us, well heck, you can even worship with us. Just don't think that you can surpass (overtake) us.

I am taking upon myself the task to point out differences, whether politically, economically, socially, and

50

developmentally, that when exposed, hopefully some thinking, some healing, some self-examination, some repentance, and above all some rectification will occur. WHY MUST THERE EXIST A YOU AND/OR ME, WHY CAN'T IT BE WE! Come to the realization that we are either ALL-ONE, or we will be ALONE!

To God be the Glory in everything I do, say, write, think and portray. When Rodney King, asked the question, "Can't we all just get along?" I believe he knew the answer, YES, we can, if the dominant's terms of implementation and existence are adhered to. Things must change in order for this Nation to get to BEING as it says "One nation under GOD, INDIVISIBLE, WITH LIBERTY AND JUSTICE FOR ALL!

So easy, yet so difficult--Love is all we need. Why do we call it Love, when at times its hurt is so strong?

AUDACITY--intrepid boldness--bold or arrogant disregard of normal restraints

LOVE--affection based on admiration, benevolence or common interests--unselfish, loyal, and benevolent concern for the good of another.

51

SURVIVAL OF THE FITTEST--DOG EAT DOG WORLD-EVEN SURVIVAL IS DESCRIBED IN SAVAGE TERMS! WHY!

One has to question the fortune of one that is established and attained through the misfortune of another, or is THAT THE WAY OF THE WORLD?

GOD Promised whatever I put my hand to do, that He would PROSPER. (3 Jn: 1, 2, Isa. 54:17) where God has given the vision, there also is provision

THE LUST OF FLESH, THE LUST OF THE EYE, AND THE PRIDE OF LIFE----WARNING, WARNING, BEWARE!

(I John 2:16) - For all that is in the world, the lust of the flesh, and the lust of the eyes, and the pride of life, is not of the Father, but is of the world.

Greed vs. Benevolence--the closed fist syndrome (until I open my hand to let go of a little of what I think I possess, how can I extend an open hand to assist another?--WHY CAN'T WE be FRIENDS--As

"WAR" Stated in the '70's, I called you, but you would not look around.

I am but a simple down to earth man, with a simple down to earth observation, of a complex, curious and what should be a non- paradoxical (not being the normal), and why situation, that continues to be the mode of operation, within a free and open-minded society.

We hold these truths (?) to be self-evident that all (?)Men, (Are all men considered to be Men?)are created equal! if so, why so many disparities, and discrepancies?

Love Ye one another, as I have Loved You (John 13:34, I Peter 1:22) - Do you truly love me, when all you do is apply one-upsmanship in all you say, apply, and do.

I loved so dearly the sermon of the Good Samaritan and its applications delivered by Bishop T.D. Jakes in the aftermath of Hurricane Katrina, especially when so many are still on their High Horses refusing to lend a hand up to the down-trodden.

53

My parents had always taught me to never think too much of myself, yet never let yourself or anyone else think or treat you lowly or less. They taught me that I am God's Child which makes me special, (1 Peter. 2:9) no matter what you think, tell or feel about me feel, contrary to the fact. God's word says it and that settles it! So as a man thinketh, so is he.

1 Peter 2:9-But ye are a chosen generation, a royal priesthood, a holy nation, a peculiar people; that ye should shew forth the praises of him who hath called you out of darkness into his marvelous light.

From the background to the Forefront--is the picture becoming too crowded too focused for comfort. From the, what can be termed the outhouse to the Big House (Whitehouse). Now they are determined to take back their Country! From what? And wouldn't "Back" be considered regression? I have been told that this is the land of opportunity, what happened to crowning the good with brotherhood from sea to shining sea?

54

If given equal opportunity, I know I can compete--"I may not get there with you, but we as a people will get to the promised land." (MLK)

Because of our love for democracy, because of our deep-seated belief that democracy transformed from thin paper to thick action is the greatest form of government on earth. (MLK)

Dec. 5, 1955--And you know my friends, there comes a time when people get tired of being trampled over by the iron feet of oppression. There comes a time, my friends, when people get tired of being plunged across the abyss of humiliation, where they experience the bleakness of nagging despair. There comes a time when people get tired of being pushed out of the glittering sunlight of life's July and left standing amid the piercing chill of an alpine November. There comes a time. (MLK)
I want to tell you this evening that it is not enough for us to talk about love, love is one of the pivotal points of the Christian face, faith. There is another side called justice. And justice is really love in

55

calculation. Justice is love correcting that which revolts against LOVE. (MLK)

Sources: Josh Gottheimer ed., RIPPLES OF HOPE GREAT AMERICAN CIVIL RIGHTS SPEECHES (New York: Basic Civitas Books, 2003)

All my life I've had to fight!--"The Color Purple". Eventually you had to allow us on the porch, but at what cost, have you only allowed us on the porch because you see the chance for photo ops, a chance to enhance yourselves, your pockets? I'm only wondering if your reasons have been selfishly motivated. They are smiling in your face, so afraid you are going to take their place! da da da dum dum dum dum dum, dum what they doing? (Paraphrase of the O'Jays)

Negative social attitudes that were so pervasive in the 60's, are even more prevalent yet cleverly covert in the 21st century.--Hate, bigotry, mistrust are all tastes that are acquired, (what was once done hidden by robes, and hoods, is now being carried out in pin-striped, suits, and the Political Elitist)

56

What is so sad in my opinion is that this nation has always taken a reactionary, rather than precautionary stance particularly in the realm of civil and race-relations. A mediocre (Don't rock the boat) action plan, which is one of NON- action, until it affects the status quo, and their means of protecting their livelihood. If not carefully handled, all are becoming as a pretty pastry with frosting that cleverly covers up the day-old foul-tasting cake of ingredients within.

We sing our National Anthem beautifully with pride, we say our Pledge of Allegiance solemnly, we even shout out proudly in the midst of international sporting events, USA, USA, USA!!! We paint a pretty picture for the whole world to see, yet if we were to gaze in the mirror of righteousness, what do we really truly see? Are we proud of how we treat our own, let alone the outside world? Can we truly say we are united, indivisible, and possess Liberty and Justice for ALL?

Happy Birthday Ty-Ty! I'm writing and dedicating this book for you, and to in some ways warn you of the world that is, in hopes that one day you will be able to write a book that your grandson will read about the world that God intended for us to inhabit, His Kingdom come on earth, as it is in heaven, true Love for one another, sharing God's love for Mankind, not governed by (Men) kind

Big business and Politics, (strange)? bedfellows of the not so curious kind. Believe me when I say I truly believe some have been taught to be friends with, but not friends of a different kind...... (Some of my best friends are....He's with me, he's one of the good ones).......Yet at the end of the day, when the lights dim, and drapes are closed, and push comes to shove, you are still regarded as that N_____o, or er! Things have to change. After all these years, after all these battles, after all the hypocrisy, after all the lies, and even truths, THINGS HAVE TO CHANGE! (Why oh why are somethings, the same, 'ol stuff, same 'ol way, same 'ol thang, yet it's a brand-new day?)

Big Mama Ruth (Labeled as a Domestic Care(Maid) specialist-- Cheated out of full Social Security benefits by the employers who smiled in Her Face, all the while lying about work quarters supposedly reported. PaPa--Brought to the brink of tears by a Rosewood-Zaragosa community center pharmacist, who felt and acted as though He were George Bush's personal Drug Czar (Not fully filling prescriptions because of government aide, or maybe even because of possible Pharmaceutical Kick-Backs).

As a nation, there are some things(stuff), collectively we all need to get off our chests. It's not that their pants are sagging, rather it's why! With the absence of light on the horizon, why make the trip (effort)? Why has the great capacity for curiosity been stymied? If the abundance there possibly killed the cat, could it be reasonable to think that the absence thereof, can lead to a fate far worse?--Dare to Dare, be of enough curiosity as to dig! DIG! Thank you, Lord, for your push, that is allowing me to shove! Have Courage, Confidence, and Commitment!

This Nation when it comes to race relations, and let's be truthful, can best be described as a Marriage, where the couple is living together, yet sleeping in separate bedrooms, simply tolerating one another, yet are illegally separated. Let the truth be known, the possibility of a national Default, and Debt-Ceiling crisis, is nothing more than a black and white issue, of Political Black Mail, or to paraphrase Whoopie

59

Goldberg of the "View", put it "This is nothing more than an unwanted Afro-American, at the "Tea-Party", issue,(Political Afro-American, Mail). It is not a what is good for the nation, democrat or republican, rich or poor issue, it all boils down to I may know what is right, but you can't tell me, I know what is white, oh excuse me what is Right.

Again, please don't piss on my leg and tell me it's raining!!!!! For this President, B Obama, it seems that bending isn't quite good enough, it seems certain facets of Government and society won't be happy until he is broken as they sip their tea from their lofty towers while exclaiming as education, opportunity, and life are going to hell in a hand basket, and or tea cup (mostly the fault of previous administration's handling of national affairs, (during the Ronald Reagan administrations rule, the Debt Ceiling was raised four time),) let them eat cake, but please don't expect to share in our sipping of the tea!

What is the pulse of the Nation, it's not what is on the Left, nor the Right, rather it what is of the spiritual persuasion, why does it have a tendency to major in the minors, and minor in the majors. Why is it in

60

Austin Texas, we vilify restaurants accused of stealing meat, even go so far as to televise their arrests complete with handcuffs, and the awarding of dirty cops whom it would seem have been given free rein when it comes to shooting first and asking questions later, knowing that their actions would eventually be cleared or no billed by a Grand Jury. C'mon Man, how long do you think we will fiddle while Rome is burning?

You seem to have the attitude, that as long as the game is played by your rules, and you are the major stock holder, holding the lion's share of the marbles, why should you be subject and held to the concept of sharing? It matters not, to possess the ability, in the absence of desire for God's Plan and opportunity.

Drink of the cup of Christ--Its contents contain the Healing of the Nation, which may be a tonic too rich to swallow for some and too bitter for others. Too much "intelligence", greed, and power in the wrong hands and minds when improperly applied can tend to make a "MONKEY" of society. An Ape can lead a group of Monkey's once he has proven that his leadership is "THE" righteous movement in the Minds of the

Monkey! "One ape is easily broken, yet a group of Monkeys may prove difficult to conquer! Take the Tea-Party, "We're taking our country back", agenda as an example, yet lately their resolve has all but imploded upon their lofty ideals and idioms.

Thank You, thank you Lord for the servants you have chosen to encourage, and push me toward the completion of this book. Thank You Lord for Manpower 2011 "Breaking New Ground", where I heard Bishop T.D. Jakes speaks on the Spirit standing up in me, with his sermon on "Stand Up to It". Thank you for Pastor Bill Winston, who taught that the Lion may not be the biggest and badest in the jungle, but he thinks he is. Thank you for Pastor Samuel Rodriguez, who taught of the olive being crushed to extract the precious oil of anointing within. Thank you for Bro. Anthony Sharpe, who during the conference not only encouraged, he also told me I was going to finish my book. So many things within the past week are working to push me toward my goal. I recently attended a viewing of the movie, The Help; it touched my heart and spirit so profoundly. One particular line from the movie that has stuck with me was, "YOU IS

KIND, you is Smart, YOU is IMPORTANT! a statement made to a child, from a servant!

When one looks into a mirror, can we really stomach what is seen? Can we really swallow, the truth of the "Pie", we have been served? In my opinion the movie served as a metaphor for the state of the present United States Government, with President Obama playing the role of the Help, and political socialites (elitist, if you will, tea parties and their factions) that of the employers. One day after viewing the movie, word comes over CNN, of a Negro Man, being beaten and run over by a truck of drunken white teenagers, out to "Get a Nigger", and in of all places, Jackson Mississippi! Some may say "It's a new day, a new time, but it seems to me in some instances, it's a new day, with old crimes and old thoughts yet in new clothing.

In order to undertake and finish this project, I must possess an audacity of courage. To do what is contrary to certain facets of society, how dare me? Every David has his Goliath, every Jonah his whale, every Christian his cross.

Black Homerun King, name put up on every negative billboard, White Pitching Legend, mistrial, and acquitted! What's Up? Can anyone say DIFFERENCES, and/or AT LEAST!!?

Chapter 5
Procrastination Turn Effort

Procrastination - To put off intentionally and usually habitually and for a reason held to be (reprehensible) as laziness, indifference to responsibility.

Turn - The action or an act of giving or taking a direction or a different direction; a change of course or posture

Reprehensible-Worthy of or deserving reprehension Reprehend-find fault with as a rebuke

Effort-A conscious exertion of physical or mental power; expenditure of energy toward particular end; forceful attempt.

To everything turn, turn, turn, there is a season, and a time and purpose under heaven- Ecclesiastes 3:1-8

Blessed is the man which hungers and thirst after righteousness, for he shall be filled. - Matthew 5:6 (King James)

God blesses those who hunger and thirst for justice, for they will be satisfied!- Matthew 5:6 (New Living Translation)

I have been given an assignment, and my steps have been ordered, yet due to dogged procrastination, to this point my assignment had remained incomplete. I have allowed what "they say" to detour my destination. I've asked God to deliver me from People of the negative ilk, and also to deliver me from ME; the ME of self-doubt, and mistrust. I've realized that I must make a TURN in my actions and thoughts and come to the desired outcome of my assignment. My Dad had a favorite saying, that being, "Once a task is begun, never leave it until it is Done"! Conceiving, Believing, and finally Achieving takes what is commonly known as "elbow grease", good old-fashioned EFFORT. I've POSSESSED the thoughts yet lacked the EFFORT TO get the task completed. I've preached the auspices and importance of NOW, while simultaneously carrying the genes of PROCRASTINATION in an era where time definitely does not stand still. I have implored upon myself, and now I do so with you as well to be patient with me, God still has an assignment on my life. I now possess a sense of urgency, and expediency of the NOW! I must get it done.

At times I have questioned why this assignment has taken so long, and then I realize that God doesn't operate within the realms of time as we understand it. Why must the journey toward racial harmony and justice, and eradication of racial inequality seemingly be a task of Herculean proportions with significant outcomes? My question is, who ordained racial injustice, and to what purpose, to what end?

Thou shalt love the lord thy god, with all thine heart, mind, and soul, and thy neighbor as thyself - Matthew 22: 37-39

I have been assigned to explore and write an expose, and review of some of my life's experiences as a BLACK MAN within this the UNITED STATES OF AMERICA. Onward with the task at hand, without further delay!

In the fall of 2013, while at a Stop Light in Austin Texas, at the intersection of Parmer Lane, and MoPac Blvd., a "Beggar" whom I'll refer to as the Johnny Cash Troubadour, due to his daily attire of Black, and his Guitar is heard shouting "Shut up Nigger", turn that

Shit off, in response to Rap Music that was emanating from a young Hispanics vehicle, two lanes over. Should I have been concerned that I may have been harmed by this deranged individual because of his perception of THUG MUSIC or the thug lifestyle or should I in this day of "OPEN CARRY" and fearing for one's life, shoot first because of my perceptions. I didn't know whether to pray for his deliverance from his ignorance, or to laugh at his asinine assumptions, or to do both. After all, "AT LEAST HE WAS WHITE"!

I've endured over five decades of ignorance and hate! How much longer will this mode of thinking continue? Some say, the more things change, the more they stay the same, yet, it is as though the SAME has underwent a SAME SHAME UPGRADE!

In the process of some reading this book, if I've ticked some off, GOOD! If I've blessed, you GREAT! My ultimate goal for writing this book has always been to stimulate thinking, reflection, and possibly repentance. Whether you've been ticked or blessed, or maybe even both, you choose the shoes or shoes that fit. The main thing is CHANGE in a positive way.

So as a man thinketh in his heart, so is He!-Prov. 23:7

Just who do you think you are? Is there any surprise of the subliminal messages being aired through modern media? Can someone tell me why Everybody Love Raymond (TV series 1996-2005), yet Everybody Hates Chris (TV series 2005-2009)?

Explore the united states of lonely pushed aside, picked on, (to be) pointed out purpose, position, passion mene, mene, tekel, upharsin-Dan. 5:23-28

Instead, you have set yourself up against the Lord of Heaven. You praised the gods of silver and gold, of bronze, iron, wood and stone, which cannot see or hear or understand. But you did not honor the God who holds in his hand your life and all your ways. Therefore, he sent the hand that wrote the inscription. This is the inscription that was written: Mene, Mene, Tekel, Parsin.

Here is what these words mean:

MENE: God has numbered the days of your reign and brought it to an end.

TEKEL: You have been weighed on the scales and found wanting.

PERES: Your kingdom is divided and given to the Medes and Persians

Dan. 5:26 - Mene can mean numbered or mina (A unit of money)

Dan. 5:27 - Tekel can mean weighed or shekel.

Dan. 5:28 - Peres(the singular of Parsin) can mean divided or Persia or a half mina or a half shekel

RECIDIVISM (NOUN) - A tendency to relapse into a previous condition or mode of behavior: especially relapse into criminal behavior (Make America Great Again)

Beware the state of this Nation, following the 2016 Presidential Election.(MAKING AMERICA GREAT AGAIN)

Hebrews 12:9- (KJV)- Furthermore we have had fathers of our flesh which corrected us, and we gave them reverence: shall we not much rather be in subjection unto the Father of spirits, and live?

COULD IT BE THAT THE YOU, YOU SEE IN THE MIRROR OF PUBLIC OPINION HELD BEFORE YOU TO REFLECT THE REAL YOU, IS NOT THE YOU, YOU PRETEND TO BE! How dare me without your permission ponder the essence of what you've been about the whole time? Dare I question the manipulative power of the real god(green) you base your greatness upon, by any means necessary! How dare ESPN Analyst, Bomani Jones, on a Nationwide Broadcast of Mike and Mike, wear a T-Shirt with a caricature depicting the CLEVELAND CAUCASIANS, with a dollar sign headband, mocking the Cleveland Indians mascot and what seems to be a reluctance to change its offensive logo. Suddenly there is an uproar on Twitter and other nationwide media. Could it be, what is good for the Gander(The Indians) aint up to snuff for the Goose(The Caucasian)? I know, that's what makes America Great! Right? Or is it another instance that screams out, AT LEAST I'M WHITE?

AFFLUENZA - IMAPONINJA

JUSTICE IMPLICATED - JUSTICE IMPLIED

I imagine one of the reasons people cling to their hates so stubbornly is because they sense, once hate is gone, they will be forced to deal with pain.--James A. Baldwin(1924-1987)

Implicate - (V.) convey (a meaning or intention) indirectly through what one says, rather than stating it explicitly

Imply - (V.) strongly suggest the truth or existence of (something not expressly stated).

Chapter 6
At Least Vs Almighty

Never in my lifetime have I experienced this nation as divided as it is at this moment. (Matt: 6:33) As we are in pursuit of the American dream, have we forgotten, or have we instituted a substitute for what really makes the dream possible. While chasing the eagle, we have lost focus especially because of the green tinting that fogs our rose color glasses. While the sun may be shining brightly, externally, internally our souls have been slipping into darkness. Everyone knows, "the freaks come out at night"! Everyone also knows that what is done in the darkness, eventually comes to light.

Capitalizing on Hate----To master the science of manipulation of the mind, as to convince yourself that you can't stand, stomach, and/or tolerate me, is so much simpler than convincing yourself that in order for this nation to move forward you must simply love me as you do yourself.(Mark 12:30,31). Yet, this I believe, if you can change your mind, you can change your world, if you can change your attitude, surely you can change your altitude, and most importantly if you can educate, you can elevate! (Hos: 4:6) Having once believed that I too was an underdog, I tend to pull for those who are in that web of erroneous belief. I've come to believe that I am of a royal priesthood, a peculiarity, if you will (1 Peter 2:9), called out of the darkness into the marvelous Light. Because of this I know, no matter what, I can do anything! I can do all things! (Phil 4:13)

Bully or Plays/Works well with others? It's my marbles, so it's my rules, or game's over.

Let's explore the unholy matrimony of the people of the United States, who couldn't be more contradictory than they are at this present moment. One hip-hop, the other preppie, one Mozart, the other the O'Jays, one poor, the other rich, one with the best that money can buy, the other barely getting by, one filet mignon, the other Vienna sausage, one loud and boisterous, the other quiet and subdued, one striving, the other complacent, one having a curious faith, the other a green faith. Without quick intervention, counselling, and a coming together of thoughts that will attain a life sustaining transfiguration, this marriage that is on life support, near flat-lining, will soon succumb to the deadly pride and prejudice virus it has been unfortunately afflicted with for ages.

INTRO--A conglomeration of thoughts, ideas, and emotions collected over the past fifty years, that I am finally able to share in writing in hopes of some semblance of healing for both writer, and reader.

Isaiah 43:1,2,7---the flood and the storm

Ecc 9:11--the battle, the race to the swift

2 Chr 7:14--If my people...

Believing, and trusting in and on the Promises of God!

John 14:1,27

Praise is what I do, continually—Ps. 34:1

"Will it go 'round in circles?"--folks who live in glass houses, shouldn't throw stones. Yet if you think of it, if you are the one who owns the factory that produces the glass, and you monopolize the gravel pit of the stones, cause, again you're holding the dynamite, while standing on top of the mountain where you have planted your flag, one would reason, you may as well throw as many pebbles, stones, and boulders as you wish, because no one is going to say anything to a man with an uncompromising persona, and dynamite in his possession to reinforce his stance, while yelling in his best Leonardo DiCaprio voice, "I'm King of the World"! **(MY GAME, MY RULES!!!!!) (ANY QUESTIONS, ANY ARGUMENTS?) (NUFF SAID)**

Will it go 'round in circles--well duh, this nation has been stuck in this pattern of complacency, mediocrity if you will at least, especially within the subject of race, and human rights during the entirety of my lifetime! Or will it fly high, like a bird up in the sky?==Every time this nation and its people have an opportunity to soar, some Elmer Fudd, simply because he perceives that ONE NOT OF HIS PERSUASION may be on the same plane, or one of a higher strata than his, decides its "a hunting we will go", and we are right back to going in circles again!

76

ROMANS 12:12, states-Rejoicing in hope, patient in tribulation; continuing instant in prayer...

Galatians 6:9, states-and let us not be weary in well doing, for in due season we shall reap, if we faint not.

Hab 2:3 - For the vision is yet for an appointed time, but at the end it shall speak and not lie, though it tarry wait for it, for it will surely come, it will not tarry.

Hab 2:4 - Behold, his soul which is lifted up is not upright in him, but the just shall live by his faith.

I don't possess diamonds or that fine clothes or jewelry, but My God is real for I can feel him in my soul.

Jeremiah 9:23-24

NYC, a place of dedication, became a place of forewarning--The cornerstone of the United States government, was destroyed on 9/11. Wake up, read the warning on the wall! "If my people which are called by my name - 2 Ch 7:14--the solution to our current woes.

I was naked, and hid myself - Gen 3:10, Matt 25:36,43 - The shame of a once Mighty Nation refusing to address the real problems of the infrastructure of this nation, has led to the crumbling of the cookie, why are we refusing to humble ourselves, and realize that we, black or white, rich or poor, cannot solve the problems of this nation until as the Chilites sang in the '70's, "There will never be any peace, until God, is at the conference table". Your nakedness has been revealed to the entire universe.

We can't as a nation continue to be "Powerful", and "Pitiful", at the same time, we will either be one or the other. We must get back to God—2 Cor 5:17 Our nation must make a choice between FEAR and FAITH. Inclusion, exclusion = NAACP, Neo-Nazi Socialist Movement, one that wants to be included in all facets of the American dream, the other dreams of an exclusive society of non-inclusion. One accused of involuntarily or deliberately using the so called "race card" in defense of their actions and reactions, the other, of a for real tho', in your face, deliberate, "At Least I'm", attitude.

Chapter 7
Exclusivity and Entitlement

It has always been so obviously clear to me, when a person for some reason or another takes on the elitist air of exclusivity, and or even aristocracy if you will! As sad as it may be in the "Home of the Brave", and the "Land of the Free", that in order to feel superior to another Human Being, we have set up a caste systems, whether admitted or not, where if you are white, you are right, and if you are black stay back. I'm not suggesting that this goes on in every situation in life, but it goes on enough as to incorporate divisions along social, economic, and racial boundaries. Some may say that I'm viewing and addressing these events, and situations as a Black Man, with a slanted and prejudiced point of view, and they are right, but more so I am viewing these situations as a Human Being created by a sovereign God, who is above reproach, and until you have walked a mile in my shoes, experienced my pain, felt my ancestors shame, of seeing wrong, and feeling helpless to do anything about those circumstance, for a moment won't you please dismount your, " High Horse of Exclusivity", and display some semblance of Humility, as to allow me to plead my case. Whether we want to believe it or not, black or white, rich or poor, status quo or radical zealot, we are all in this thing called Life within the United States, under one God(?), torn apart in an indivisible(?) Nation, TOGETHER (?)! Why can't we be friends?

While growing up I often felt that if I didn't confront a situation, it would simply go away, but as with the Bully who takes your lunch money daily, if not finally reprimanded, and confronted, the bully will continue to fester, as a cancer, and in most instances his actions will only get worse, to the point where you just don't want to go to learn, grow, or even attend school! United States this is my Bully Confrontation, my moment to say, "enough is enough"! I am not only pointing the finger of blame in the other direction, for I realize that sometimes our greatest opposition and enemy is "IN-A-ME"! I truly believe that charity does begin at home, and that I can't truly embrace you, until I can truly Love myself. "I must work the works of Him that sent me while it is day, for the night comes that no man can work." I have picked up my cross, to bear the responsibility in somehow removing the scales covering the eyes of justice, and equality. Yes,

United States, we have major league issues, that our ivory towers can't shield us from, raise us above, nor blind us to.

Exclusivity--Serena Williams' $10,500 fine for "Unsportsmanlike Behavior" for berating and "cussing", a Lines official during the 2009 U.S. Open Tennis Women's Semifinal match, as compared to "Roger Federer's, $1,500 fine for Cussing an official the next day, yet as Patrick McEnroe, Tennis Analyst for ESPN Sports puts it Roger has always been a class act. Someone please explain to me, how one could be able to "Cuss", someone with class! I by no means condone Serena's actions on that day, but I do understand. Sometimes enough is enough. Why Should one's loss of composure in a public arena, be deemed, any worse than another's, or does f------!, hold more value than a S-----!, in the arena, of Classy (?) Cuss Words? I was appalled to hear one talk show host(ess) make reference to Serena's actions as "You can take the girl out of Compton, but you can't take the Compton out of the....You know the rest." Why at that point didn't the talk show hostess realize, that she was only being used by the status quo(network executives), to say, to put out there what they wanted to express yet couldn't, for fear of being deemed as socially and

81

politically incorrect, and that she is only being used as a pawn(puppet) in the game of the talk show genre. Why could she have not given Serena, the benefit of the doubt, and moved on? What she did at that particular time and moment was reinforce, the notion of what has been described as the "Crab Mentality"! prevalent within the Negro Race. Please stop attempting to boost your ratings at the expense of another's misfortunes. You owe Serena an apology, "How You Doing"?

Chapter 8
Can't Buy Me Love

Can't buy me Love--Imagine if you will, having experienced the top while existing on the bottom, then imagine never experiencing the bottom while living on top. Money can buy one quite a variety of things, yet it will never afford or guarantee one's acceptance. White Money does not equate to White Entitlement. I've discovered my starting point!

Before discovering, and discussing others, I first must observe myself, from the standpoint of a mortal, and moreover spiritual "DUMBASS"!

Greatest Warrior of all recorded time:

- David, of Goliath fame

- Greatest Peacekeeper of all recorded time - MLK Jr.

- Greatest Political (Over comer) Accomplisher of all U.S. recorded time - Barack H. Obama

- Greatest Spiritual and Human Leader, and sacrifice of all time - Jesus Christ

Dumb - being unable to move and/or operate under self-motive, or manipulation

Ass - a servant, beast of burden.

I've got to do what I have been assigned to do. I must work the works of Him
(John 9:4)

I must arrive from the point of "AT LEAST", to my destination of "At Most"!

From a place of Disenchantment, to a place of Humility. (2 Chr. 7:14) (Rom. 12:3).

Black (Man), plus White (Money), may equal white cars, white clothes, white suites, and maybe even a White (House), yet it will never equate, at least in their minds, and their world to white privileges, and white social strata. In other words, at the end of the day, you are still considered to be that Black Man, who happens to have money, while they are if nothing else "At

Least", white, and that in their mindset is equivalent to "greater than".

Realize again that you just happen to be a Black Man with money, of which they have already devised schemes to separate you from said money, while attaining their "rightful share". Can't buy me Love! Be as the eagle who worries not of the circumstance of the wind, But it uses the wind (its troubles) to propel itself to greater heights far above the circumstances, where it can be heard as it proudly proclaims, in the words of Johnny Nash, in his chart topping song, "I can see clearly now, the rain is gone, gone are the sad clouds, that had me down, it's gonna be a bright sunshiny day'!

Teetering on the edge of the High diving board at the deepest end of the pool, fear is telling me to turn around, that I can't do it, and why did you even dare to climb, and then a greater spirit, and a greater faith quietly whispers, "This is your jump off point, your cross-roads, choose ye this day to jump off, dumb ass!

Dumb: Having to be directed by outside forces and influences Ass: A beast of burden

Thank you, Pastor Lance Watson, for your analogy of the Stamp (stick to your assignment, until you get to desired destination), and the Mighty Oak (a nut that decided to hold his ground). Thank you for your push at my Jump-off point. The who, what, where, and why the why--to impose upon the supposed (imaginary) (members only) Ivory Towers of privilege, in spite of and because of!

This book intends to explore the who, what, when, and whys of society, during my past, present, and future existence.

The Racial Relations standing over the years, can best be described as a forced Marriage of coexistence where one party within the relationship is present yet absent, being tolerated, yet unappreciated, a hemorrhoid, that preparation H, court ordered integration, affirmative action, etc. only serves as a temporary balm.

Just a simple man, with a simple observation, of an overly complicated capital life issue of Race-(Non) Relations within this the United States of America. "Poor Kids need to work, and Black People can't think for themselves", ala Newt Gingrich, and Herman Cain. (Criminal Justice)—48- Hrs. Murder Mystery--The accused Tim Masters(served over nine years for murder), the accuser Lead Police Officer Jim Brodrick--Withheld evidence collected by him, local officers, and the FBI,   lead prosecutors later reprimanded only after being promoted to Judge positions.   Another case of being proven innocent through DNA technology not available at the time of the crime. A case of an overzealous Cop, in a rush to justice in a small town within a nation of Liberty and Justice for all.

Thank you, Father God, for the Heroes you have placed in my life. How to react when your "White Card", is no longer accepted,

"Ye though I walk through the valley of the shadow of death, I will fear no evil, for thou art with me....Psalms 23

Chosen to be Challenged, Challenged to be Blessed, Blessed to be Chosen.

I'll not allow more to be put upon you than you can bear - I Cr. 10:13

The day my son was born, I wept, knowing what would be before him, next to him in the hospital nursery was a newborn Caucasian baby, and I thought to myself, "at least he's white". Why such a vast gulf between the Haves and the perceived Have nots, why in the home of the brave, compassion rarely exists between opposite spectrums of the stick". Why can't we be friends?

From unconditional acceptance (MAN), to conditional tolerance (MAN), to unconditional acceptance (GOD). The greatest threat to a common Mankind, has proven to be alienated mankind. From satisfied with the Mediocre, to striving for the so-called unattainable. Life is a song worth singing, why don't we sing it? i.e. Teddy Pendergrass
During a time of near recession, children starving in eastern Africa, home foreclosures at an all-time high, now we are experiencing today near riots in malls all across the U.S., for a pair of $200 Air Jordan Basketball Shoes!! Come on man, where are your priorities, let alone your values.

I've learned to respect the difference between implication, and application. In other words, to coin a phrase "Just Do it". One is to think, and the other is to do. There exists within this nation a gulf that is too immense too big, I almost used the word gap, but this thing is too massive, a gulf between Needy and Greedy. The hurt and guilt that may be felt while experiencing certain situations from an outside perspective is only an implication that compassion is

88

working within me. It's only when I'm moved to do something to right a wrong that application will begin to be adhered to. Be careful of the mirrors that you by chance peer into, especially if those mirrors are cracked, smashed, or broken. Joy and Pain--They're both one in the same, i.e., Frankie Beverly, and Maze. (2 Tim: 1:7-fear)   (Psa. 30:5-weeping). Observing this nation's reflection through a broken mirror. Choosing only to see what satisfies one's ego.

WE ARE ONE--No matter what or how you feel. All things are relative. I Need You, You Need Me, we're all a part of God's Body, it is His will that every need be supplied. Take time to think of how all things play an integral part in all things. All things work together for the good....(Romans 8:28). Realize what is required of you (Luke 12:48). Think if there were no White, why would there be Black, would you be rich, without the poor, would there be a straight, had there not been a curve, would there be excess, had there existed not lack, would there be a slave without a master, would there be joy without pain, would there be a calm, had not a storm been present, would there be heaven, without a hell, would there be war, without the possibility of peace, would there be night, if there were no day. We are one!!!!

The over/under quotient, one can't overcome, until one undergoes. There is no in, without an out, no over without an under, no light, without a dark, and no true life without a death. Stop the Bleeding--(Isa. 64:6). This nation is bleeding, and it can't stop without us touching the hem of His Garment--(Mark 5:28-30)

When you feel that you've gone as low as you can go, the only viable direction to head is DEEPER to discover new Heights! To be a success, one must realize sooner rather than later, that procrastination is the arch enemy of progress. Procrastination has been the pallbearer of many notions, ideas, and lives full of promise. What are we waiting on? Can't buy me love.

Chapter 9
Lord, Lift Us Up from Negativity

The cycle of enhancement in essence is the give and take, the out and in, the pour out, the pour in, the what God has given me, I want to share with you, and what God has given you, please share with others. We on the contrary live by the "I've got mine, you get yours", theory of prosperity in life. Holy Spirit, come on in the room, dwell within this nation, and above all dwell within our lives. "Know ye not, that ye are the temple of God, and that the spirit of God resides within (I Corth. 3:16).

Our mission should be to focus beyond the Cross. "Pick up your cross and follow me daily....

"God shed his grace on Thee"! And Crowned thy good, with brotherhood, (?) from sea to shiny sea!!!! I understand the grace, yet it would be hard to conceive, God's Favor being bestowed upon this Nation, if ever. The qualities of Righteousness, necessary to qualify for God's Favor are sorely evident.

"Inheritance" - Family, Fairness, Forgiveness, and Faith, all fulfilled through Love (Prov. 13:22), Knowledge (Hosea 4:6)

The Who--sociologist, theologist, politician, humanitarian the what-righteousness and consciousness, the when-now and forever, the where-earth! Thy Will be done on Earth, as it is in Heaven! Pres. Obama's Nobel Peace Prize--"He went unto his own, and his own knew him not", GOP Party Pres.--What has he done? Dallas District Attorney Watkins hated for Doing the Right (Un-white) thing! AA Statesmen article 10/10/09.

Even when I win, in some minds, I lose, and then when I lose, I win--to the chagrin of some talk show hosts, and GOP constituents, who celebrated the U.S. not getting the 2016 Olympic Games, what some considered a personal defeat for Obama, were aghast to learn a few weeks later, the world bestowed upon the Trumpeter of Hope, the Nobel Peace Prize. Hope, a key component of Faith. Don't celebrate my perceived downfall too quickly, for what God has for me is for me. Health, Education, and Welfare---all boil down to what the status quo of the United States value more than anything else in this universe, and that would be "Money", one of my all-time favorite musical vocal group is the O'Jay's, and in the mid-70's, they had a hit single titled, "For the Love of Money", that had lyrics that rang so true even today, when it comes to the majority's and minority's views for that matter and their takes on money, greed, and selfishness, when you have some time look up and listen to the tune on You Tube. This song tells you flatly there is almost nothing that an individual wouldn't do for money----filthy lucre, the love of money is the root of all evil. Life, Liberty, and the pursuit of Happiness, (which in this society equates to MONEY).

Where is Daddy? Absence of our families, how can the one who is supposed to be a role model, be said model, when said role-model, has no time, no effort, no drive? Why? Could this have been planned? How do the rich get Richer? Why do the Heathen rage? Ps: 2:1

"Education of the mind, without education of the Heart, is no Education at all" - Aristotle

"The roots of education are bitter, but the fruit is sweet." Aristotle

93

The sobering effect of Drunkenness - is there such a thing as a hangover from reality? Within the fog of drunkenness, speaks the voice of clarity. While not perfectly clear of mind and thought, your true essence is sometimes spilt on unsuspecting fabric of life. Sometimes Drunkenness speaks in unwatered down, unthought out, and unadulterated soulfulness and or soullessness.

The reality of spirituality vs. mortality - why do we continue to treat the Almighty God as a mortal "Santa Claus", when He is the essence of life, and the Omnipotent Spiritual Being--The God Head! Will we always be destined to be a people, who is governed by a state of one-ups-man ship? Is it and will it always be about "the" god, Money, or will we ever come to the reality that we are about our heavenly father's business, ONE LOVE, One Faith, One GOD! "THE" GOD. Explore the Nike Commercial, "Break to Build" - God has the order of breaking Bread--"HE" takes you, He Blesses you, He Breaks you, and He will use you!--Old Game Show, "What's My Line"--Will the real Black Men please stand up! When will the forgiven, forgive?

When will the Proud so consumed within pride, clearly teach of Pride, its benefits, and its downfalls?

Everyone wants to be a Doctor, yet no one wants to take the necessary medicine. Everyone wants to learn, yet no one wants to be taught. Teach our children a value system that is not dependent upon Money. Trey Songz--I want the money, cars, and the clothes, I just want to be successful. Come on Man!

Please read and meditate on these poems:

To travel the path least chosen--Robert Frost--the poem Invictus--My head is bloodied but unbowed.

I don't wanna do wrong, but it's been so long, I just can't help myself'--GK & the Pips. Why does the black hairy caterpillar cross the busy highway? Everybody's talking, yet no one is communicating. A nation of political correctness (?) leads to thirteen killed in Killeen's Ft. Hood! A nation of racial incorrectness? leads to unknown numbers killed daily--Has our nation become numb to the killing, the lying, the social, physical, mental, and moral consequences attributed to correctness.

As though you really care! Marie Antoinette famously stated, "Let them eat cake", Former First Lady, Barbara Bush stated "Those people are better off. Should I have been outraged by your blasé' response to the devastation that was Hurricane Katrina's effect upon New Orleans and its residents, and your slow, almost mediocre reaction. The Bible says that "Vengeance is Mine, saith the Lord".

Shaken to silence, silenced to Shake--70's O'jays - Money vs. 21st century's Birdman's--I've got Money to Blow--Different trains of thought, one bent on blowing (living for the moment), the other bent on investing (living for the moment while taking stock of the future), and warning of the pitfalls of money. Purpose to educate, and enlighten (none is so blind, as he who will not see, eyes wide shut).

Segregation - a reality of the oppressed, enforced by the oppressor.

Integration - a socio-political, sound bite, geared to pacify the thinking of those who feel the sting of those segregated, and oppressed terms to be examined.

Gentrification, pacification, fair housing, and labor practices.

Nigger

96

This should prove to be one of the most intriguing segments of this chapter. I will attempt to dissect, and review a word that is so easily spewed, in an effort to denigrate, humiliate, and   for lack of a better term "low-rate", an entire race, and awkwardly enough validate, and elevate the self-image of its user. To use a by-line from a Tyler Perry Play, thanks for your help, but "I can do bad all by myself".

Please understand that there are two entirely different cultural meanings and connotations for that word Nigger!   There are also two pronunciations. Nigger and Niggah are two opposites that exist on opposite ends the same axis.

That Nigger--MLK (Nobel Prize Recipient, Civil Rights Advocate), Ben Carson (Heart Surgeon), Denzel Washington (Actor), Serena and Venus Williams (Tennis Pros), Tiger Woods (Golfer), Barack Obama(Politician, Humanitarian, President of the United States), Paul Roberson (Humanitarian, actor). When given the opportunity, That Nigger can, and will despite all of your most profound negative efforts, excel.

Niggah--spade, spook, dogg, my boy, jigga, despite your ill-founded, ill-thought out efforts, they only will serve to further denigrate, and destroy.

97

While growing up in East Austin, Texas whenever I would hear a person other than a Negro, refer to anyone of the Negro Race, as a "Nigger", I was sickened, angered, and left in a state of wonderment as to why one would want to lower the esteem, and self-image of another. As I grew older depending upon whom the term was coming from, I would either be bolstered, or be embarrassed. Allow me to explain, 60's and 70's "Nigger", 90's and 21st century Niggah!

So as a man thinketh in his heart, so is he!-Prov. 23:7

Rev N. Bacon, in a sermon during an Easter Celebration, stated that we can't truly bury the hatchet if we continue to leave the handle exposed, to pull the hatchet back out when offended, or deemed necessary. Who keeps throwing a life preserver to this term continually after it has been repeatedly thrown into the abyss of crude terminologies, when it has outlived its so-called "usefulness"? Let the wheat and the tare grow together! (Matt: 13:30) Jigga what, Jigga who? Once a seed is planted, and properly tended, the produce whether good or bad will flourish. We can either fertilize or eradicate.

98

One politician, Earl Butz, in 1976, famously made the statement when asked why there were so few black Republicans, and I am paraphrasing, answered "the only things the coloreds are looking for in life and I'm paraphrasing, "If you want to keep the Nigger happy, you needed only three items, A)" A tight pu----, B) Loose shoes, and C) A warm place to sh--!" This may very well be true of any Nigger, white or black! What are your thoughts 45?

You meant it for my bad, but God Has always and is continually working it out for my good! Every time I heard that word used in hatred, disgust, and disdain, it only acted as a Booster Shot, you know, it stings at inception, yet bolsters the immune system upon its absorption. With every Booster shot, I became stronger, and more immune to the vile ravages of Racism, and Fear that word served, and more determined to help in its eradication, the word, the thinking and non-thinking behind its use. That term helped to "Lift me up where I belong".

Our youth have laid claim to and exclusive use of the term, despite its negative connotations. How ironic, Nigger lifts me, and Niggah disgusts and sickens me. The one, who wanted to hurt, helped, and the one who should be wanting to help, hurts. How

99

can you lay claim and so easily justify the use of Niggah, as a term of endearment, and or even pride? Wake up. The enemy doesn't have to kill us, if we are killing ourselves, not only physically, but mentally, and spiritually. Are you the new boisterous "Klan"? Are you, to coin a phrase, a poet (Of death, destruction, and demoralization) and don't even know it? Wake up!! Stop hitting the snooze button, desiring more pointless dreams in what is a pointless sleep! While you are sleeping the world is passing you by. Your baggy saggy pants, your Gold grill, your low SAT's, your high Prison entries, when will you wake up! The Hip done Hopped, the Bling done blanged, and stop the hating because the games of mindless self-gratification, self-indulgence, and self-destruction, are rapidly coming to an end. "Ask not for whom the bell tolls, if you don't hastily open you heart, mind, and soul, please seriously consider, and realize it is tolling for thee."

Whatevah!"---"You know what I'm sayin'?---When you've been told for so long, that you can't, and/or you aren't, or they are, or can! Mindsets begin to form whether purposely or subconsciously. "So as a Man Thinketh, so is He"(Prov. 23:7). To use the terms, whatever, and you know what I'm sayin is true indication that you are ignorant as to what you are attempting to say and or think, or you simply lack the capacity to adequately convey what you are attempting to get across. In the lyrics of an Envogue song, it states, to Free your mind and the rest will follow, be color blind, don't be so shallow".

Chapter 10
After the Verdicts Were Announced, Alchemies

God bless the Davis Family for their proclamation of Forgiveness in the matter of the defendant in the Loud Music Murder Trial in Florida. It would seem that getting a Jury Pool of Mr. Dunn's Peers is exactly what happened in this case. Jury members who undoubtedly think and feel exactly as Mr. Dunn. With the interpretation of how the law in Florida applies in this and the infamous Zimmerman case, it would appear to be plausible, that anyone can and will get away with murder, with the "right" representation, and the "right" jury! It appears something is wrong with our interpretation and system of "With Liberty, and Justice for All"! Please pray for the strength and healing of this nation it's criminal justice system, and the Davis Family!

In the Davis Case, Juror Number 8 stated "Sometimes doing NOTHING is the RIGHT THING to do, Dunn is a good guy! Wow!

To be of relevance, we must all ask ourselves what our relevancy is building in the Kingdom of God. To be relevant, we must come to a point of realization that if my fellow man hasn't recognized the importance of his purpose in the Kingdom, and I haven't been of assistance along the way, where is the value of said relevance. We must all benefit from the fellowship of Mankind. For you to increase, at some point I must decrease! In the Kingdom, Edification is an optimum qualification. Has your life any relevancy, are you relevant, have you spread some Love today?

Stand Your Ground Thugs

These Thugs have recently turned out to be Immature, impotent cowards whose only hardness is derived from the "Cold Steel" in their hands, and their false sense of superiority! Cold Steel legalized through mis thought, misguided legislation, whether they be a common citizen or those who are sworn to keep the peace and uphold the law. A coward is a coward, and a thug is a thug!

THUG- A violent person, especially a criminal!

Urban Definition- someone who is going through struggles, has gone through struggle A cruel or vicious ruffian, robber or murderer.

THE FEAR OF THE LORD IS THE BEGINNING OF WISDOM AND KNOWLEDGE, BUT A FOOL DESPISES WISDOM AND INSTRUCTION—Prov. 9:10

There are Perils in not Recognizing the TRUE THUGS!

MY PEOPLE PERISH (ARE DESTROYED) FOR A LACK OF KNOWLEDGE–Hosea 4:6

ALCHEMY–The medieval forerunner of chemistry, based on the supposed transformation of matter. It was concerned particularly with attempts to convert base metals into gold or to find a universal elixir seemingly magical process of transformation, creation, or combination.

BILL OF SALE--serves as legal evidence that full consideration has been provided in a transaction and is usually required to be under seal.

FOOL'S GOLD--a brassy yellow mineral, especially pyrite, that can be mistaken for gold. Someone who is in love with someone who is only using them or taking advantage of them.

Romans 13:12-14--The night is far spent; the day is at hand: let us therefore cast off the works of darkness and let us put on the armor of light. Let us walk honestly, as in the day; not rioting and drunkenness, not in chambering and wantonness, not is strife and envying. But put ye on the Lord Jesus Christ, and make not provision for the flesh, to fulfil the lusts thereof.

Matthew 20:16--So the last shall be first, and the first last: for many be called, but few chosen.

Hebrews 12:1-3 (NIV)Therefore, since we are surrounded by such a great cloud of witnesses, let us throw off everything that hinders and the sin that so easily entangles. And let us run perseverance the race marked out for us, fixing our eyes on Jesus, the pioneer and perfecter of faith. For the joy set before him he endured the cross, scorning its shame and sat down at the right had of the throne of God. Consider

Him who endured such opposition from sinners, so that you will not grow weary and lose heart.

Galatians 6:9--(KJV)--And let us not be weary in well doing, for in due season we shall reap, if we faint not

Don't awaken me from this Pleasant Dream of possible equality and opportunity, because, for too long I've known the REALITY of your foot on my throat, choking out my DREAM, that is my constant NIGHTMARE. Yet for change to finally come about, I (we) must AWAKEN! It is so Ironic to now watch the stark reality of those that prosper at the expense of those they have perceived as weak and unworthy of the so-called American Dream, watch as those once denied AWAKENING! Some still feel that there must not exist the notion of an inclusive reality of opportunity for ALL, and fruition of the deprived, and neglected Dreams. How then do we pacify, the clamoring uproar of those who are justly aching for a real taste of life, and life abundancy? I've got it, let's, after the Emancipation Proclamation hand those freed slaves, an Alchemy, and let's make them think that they are now a part of a Nation of Liberty and Justice for ALL.

Let's promise the freed slave, 40 acres and a Mule! Yeah that ought to keep them happy for a while. Please research this concept initiated in post-civil war days of the 1800's, and you will find some of its concepts are in effect today as we look at the advent of GENTRIFICATION in many urban areas of the United States Today in the 21st Century.

GENTRIFICATION - The process of wealthier residents moving to an area, and the changes that occur due to the influx of wealth. As wealthier inhabitants move into an area already populated with lower-income residents, the neighborhood begins to change as well. The restoration and upgrading of deteriorated urban property by middle-class or affluent people, often resulting in displacement of lower-income people.

Alright the 40 acres and a Mule only pacified for a short while, so what do we do now to calm the uproar for equality? Eureka, they've come up with their own pacifier, and it's delivered to them at the march on Washington for Equality delivered by their modern-day Moses; Martin Luther King Jr.! That Pacifier has

107

been in effect for over fifty years and is known as the "I HAVE A DREAM" speech so eloquently delivered by Dr. King of his Dream for his People to reach the promised land of opportunity, and equality. 50 years later, some are still happy that the Dream is still only a Dream. We as a Nation must WAKE UP and make the Dream, Reality! Put away the ALCHEMIES of Mules and Dreams, and distance ourselves from the AT LEAST! Was, "We hold these TRUTHS to be self-evident, that all men are created equal" not intended for all Men? Take a look around and tell me while looking at the state of this Union, that the previous declaration is one of truth?

Chapter 11
Forgive Me, Cracked Bell

Forgive me if I don't completely share in your demonstrative display of National Allegiance, and Pride. Please allow me to explain the reasoning as it pertains to the previous statement:

TAINT--to affect or be affected by contamination or corruption.

PATRIOTISM--the act of support and allegiance to one's country.

DENIAL--a refusal, a disavowal, an unwillingness to believe or acknowledge.

My degree of Patriotism has been irrevocably affected by two monstrous factors; TAINT and DENIAL. There remains DIFFERENCES in those wounded, and saved, and unsaved, attributed to a Nation whose Allegiance from its Citizens is an unspoken expectation, and how the same Nation displays its reciprocity to those affected disproportionately. I have every right bestowed each citizen of this nation. Should I not have the right to return what is given, or should I continue to have head bowed while in the presence of your ill-conceived false notion of superiority, no matter the situation and simply shuffle along, dancing to the tune you have arranged to benefit your rhythm only?

COULD IT BE DUE MY HUE?

Some may ask, who am I to whine and moan, about the state of affairs, and I will answer, I'm a Citizen of the United States of America, a citizen who recognizes HEALING and REPENTANCE is sorely needing to take place to assure and insure according to its creed; LIBERTY, and JUSTICE for ALL, for the LEAST, and for the MOST! We must distance ourselves from being a nation with a notion of, if you're Tinted, then you are possibly Tainted .

COULD IT BE DUE MY HUE that I'm usually considered Guilty before proven Innocent

COULD IT BE DUE MY HUE that I am often fired before hired

COULD IT BE DUE MY HUE that you feel that I should be satisfied with the crumbs from the master's table

COULD IT BE DUE MY HUE that I must answer unwarranted questions in a Nation Of Justice for All

COULD IT BE DUE MY HUE that in Florida I can justifiably be murdered by your STAND YOUR GROUND LAW VIGILANTLY as I'm guilty of WWB (Walking While Black)

COULD IT BE DUE MY HUE, that in Austin Texas, I can be justifiably murdered as I sleep in my vehicle, and I fit the description, dang, SWB (Sleeping While Black)

COULD IT BE DUE MY HUE, that you can legally rip me off with a smile via Pay Day, and Title Loans

It is due my hue, that I don't feel the Allegiance that you do! All my life those of my HUE have been treated as the unwanted step-child, left out of the Founding Father's Will, with very little chance of future inheritance.

Is it due my hue that you pre-judge, clutch your purses, and lock your car doors at the mere sight of me?

Is it due my hue that you consider me ARROGANT, when I consider your actions toward me, without knowing me, IGNORANT? Imagine my GUMPTION, to question your AUDACITY!

So, bear with me, if it appears that I don't share in your enthusiasm while reciting the Pledge of Allegiance, and singing the Star-Spangled Banner, that to many are hypocritical of what this Nation stands for, meant for SOME, and not shared by ALL!   AT LEAST I'M WHITE! Brother Please! Imagine my Life, many segments to my dismay. COULD MY HUE, BE THE CLUE!!??

Cracked Bell, Cracked Liberty!

Getting Better than what is Given (Servitude)

Supply (Slaves) and Demand (Slave Masters-Then and Now)

Correct me if I am wrong, but am I to assume that the Constitution, the Bill of Rights, and the Liberty

112

Bell rang true for all citizens of the nation under One God, The United States of America, both Black and White? Is the clause and cause of Life, Liberty, and the Pursuit of Happiness applied equally?

Cracked-adj. damaged and showing lines on the surface from having split without coming apart crazy, insane

Bell-noun. an object, typically made of metal and having the shape of a deep inverted cup widening at the lip, that sounds a clear musical note when struck, typically by means of a clapper inside.

Liberty-noun. the state of being free within society from oppressive restrictions imposed by authority on one's way of life, behavior, or political views.

CRACKED LIBERTY BELL-The Liberty Bell is an iconic symbol of American Independence, located in Philadelphia Pennsylvania. Cast with the lettering "Proclaim LIBERTY throughout all the land unto all the inhabitants thereof"!

What is Cracked is often Condemned, exposed as being unworthy to be inhabited

How can a Free Nation run To and Fro, simultaneously?

Surviving a MUTABLE NATION solely through the GRACE OF AN IMMUTABLE GOD! A nation that has allowed Love to be replaced with LUST! Thy Will be done on Earth, as it is in Heaven

Rom. 4:13-15

How can one escape/flee a stiff necked, hard hearted Kingdom, only to establish an elitist hard hearted, stiff necked Nation?

Only those that claim the BLACK LIVES MATTER agenda has gotten out of control have more than likely only seriously considered that their lives exclusively were the only lives that mattered, maintaining their, let's be honest, snobbish, let them eat cake, blasé, status quo state of BEING!

I'm not stating that one segment of society is exclusively to blame. I am, truth be told, stating that one segment OVERWHELMINGLY represents the root cause.

Think about it, OPPORTUNITY DENIED, is OPPORTUNITY LOST! Rage against the Machine! CRACKED!

"Ignorance is the Night of the Mind. A night without a moon or stars"-Confusions

"You can't Crown Me, until you Cross me"- TD Jakes

It is not the question of EQUALITY, rather it is the FEAR of being surpassed, and of possibly receiving what has been hatefully, and selfishly blindly given.

RIGHTEOUS INDIGNATION, while awaiting RIGHTEOUS RECIPROCITY, as some are fearful of the Karma that possibly awaits.

Tiring of being your Scapegoats, your Whipping Boys, your Excuses for your frustration, your shortcomings, your Guilt! You, the AT LEAST, Pillars of Society! CRACKED!

"To the Living we owe respect. To the dead we owe the Truth"-Voltaire. It matters not the fineness of the texture, nor the lay of the cloth that covers the ugliness of the Heart, the true nature which lies within cannot forever be concealed, and the truth shall be revealed!

To know the quality of a car's engine, one simply needs to listen to the quality of its idling hum. Listen to an individual's conversation and it will reveal what is of one's character. For with the mouth, the contents of the heart are revealed. What does your Hum reveal about you? Are you the quiet consistent strong hum of a Jaguar XJ, or are the backfiring muffler of a broken down empty Hoopty?

Why in Heaven's name are we still in the state of racial discrimination and inequality? Why are some entitled to AFFLUENZA as others are afflicted with LACKLOCKANDKEYENZA? CRACKED!

116

To peer through the Looking Glass which represents the Future, one must first honestly evaluate the reflection captured in the Mirror of the Present with retrospect and repentance while divulging the Truth and nothing but the Truth, that is far removed from the Convenient Truth. In light of racial tensions, and national disharmony, it would stand to reason, that there remains far too many unwilling to admit to and rectify the dastardly sins of the True Past upon which this nation was built, and in some cases continues to operate. It would seem so strange that so many are so fascinated with the Paranormal, while Reality is currently stranger than fiction. CRACKED!

ALIW, a state of mind, a state of CRACKED BEING, which is void of Moral Value, and unconscientiously subjected by the Color of Green, and the retention thereof that has become their god! CRACKED!

To dispel, dispense, and incarcerate that which is misunderstood and feared! i.e., Trail of tears, Dred Scott, Japanese Interment, etc., legacy of a Free

117

Nation, that comes at a price too steep for too many, Only in America. CRACKED!

THOSE best fitted to acquire power are least fitted to exercise said power. CRACKED!

To mend the CRACKS.-"And He made it again another"-Reckoning of a Nation, through the cleansing power of the Blood of Jesus Christ! We must collectively invite the return of RIGHTEOUSNESS.

Using antiquated Laws, twisted to fit dubious Hip Pocket Prosecution! Hiding in Plain Sight! The Murderers of Tamir Rice, Michael Brown, Sandra Bland, etc. caught on video, yet are exonerated because apparently what we saw ain't what we saw. AFFLUENZA murderer flees from prosecution, only to be slapped on the wrist! 2 1/2 Men, HIV infected actor admitted to knowingly sleeping unprotected with multiple partners, yet there is little to no uproar! Pro Football player whose uniforms are Black, and Gold accused of RAPE, yet is celebrated as one of the NFL'S BEST, while another is vilified for Animal Cruelty, and another for Domestic Violence! How quickly, and different

118

the mindset for JUSTICE in these cases. Could it be a preponderance issue of ALIW and you're not! CRACKED!

Walter Scott, dentist accused of killing Otis the Lion, is more vilified that the State Government of Michigan who allowed the Lead Poisoning of its drinking water in the city of Flint, upon its citizens whose population is majority Black, yet not the uproar that should be within the United States of America. Is it that these citizens are considered COLLATERAL DAMAGE, within the Money Game of America, after all the States Government quickly cleared the water problem that affected the Auto Industry from the same river! CRACKED!

BEWARE! The Higher the Heights, the Deeper the Depths.

Fear of the American Dream! Crumbling reality for some! A perpetual Dream with little to no chance of Fruition for others. Yet for the ones of Reality Achieved, comes fear that the false Dreamers are AWAKENING! UNITED STATES wilt thou be made whole? CRACKED!

From the Headlines, ADULTSIZED TEEN infected with AFFLUENZA! How can the UNadultisized, Adults teach and be an example for the **ADULTISIZED** Man-Child? That would be akin to the Blind leading the Blind, yet SOME are allowed to use this as a defense in a court of Law! CRACKED!

We will never be United as long as we possess a mindset where one's Nightmare is at the expense of another's Dream. Where ones Freedom is at the expense of another's enslavement, where one's opulence is at the expense of another's squalor. The scales of Human Dignity, and Morality must be balanced!

For whom the BELL tolls, surely it is not for "THEE"! Tommie Smith's and John Carlos' gloved clenched raised fist during the awards ceremony during the 1968 Summer Olympics in Mexico City, rang truer of LIBERTY than that of the cracked BELL fame!

How does one flee a Monarchy, and run to establish a Nation, and then deny the Freedom that they so desperately were seeking for themselves, to an entire sect of its people? CRACKED

WRONG/RIGHT has been considered Right for so long, as that RIGHT/RIGHT is considered WRONG! CRACKED!

Proverbs 14:12-There is a way which seemeth right unto man, but the ends thereof are the ways of Death

LOVE IS ALL WE NEED! "If my people, who are called by my name, will humble themselves and pray and seek my face and turn from their wicked ways, then I will hear from Heaven, and I will forgive their sin and will heal their land"-2 Chronicles 7:14

Our Nation is in dire need of a Rebirth

Jeremiah says in the book of Jeremiah 18:3-4, Then I went down to the Potter's House, and there he was, making something at the wheel. And the vessel that he made of clay was marred in the hand of the

Potter; so, he MADE IT AGAIN INTO ANOTHER vessel, as it seemed good to the potter to make.

We as a Nation must admit that we are as the clay, marred, in the hands of THE POTTER, and the POTTER is not pleased with His Product! We must allow THE POTTER to put us back together again!

Before you take pride in the differences and the moniker of AT LEAST I'M WHITE, please consider Matthew 25:40-The King will reply, "Truly I tell you, whatever you did for one of the least of these brothers and sisters of mine, you did for me."

Matthew 25:45-"He will reply, Truly I tell you, whatever you did not do for one of the least of these, you did not do for me."

A CRACKED NATION in need of the Potter's Wheel and Touch, to be reshaped, reformed, and put back together again! We need Repentance, and the ability to allow Christ back into our nation, our souls, our lives! All WE NEED is Liberty, and

122

Justice for ALL! All we NEED is found in the true meaning of that four-letter word! LOVE!

Chapter 12
Thugs Ride

Judge not, that ye be not judged 2. For with what judgement ye judge, ye shall be judged, and with what measure ye mete, it shall be measured to you again 3. And beholdest thou the mote that is in thy Brother's eye, but considerest not the beam that is in thine own eye?--Matthew 7:1-3(KJV)
THUGS RIDE

Some will say THUGS RIDE AROUND WITH BOOMING SYSTEMS, some will say THUGS POSSESS SYSTEMS, BOOMING, i.e., CEO's of collapsed Mortgage Schemes, which receive government sanctioned bailouts, corporate heads of Payday and Title Loan Legal Loan Shark corporations. Some will see THUGS of inside market trading adorned with pinstriped suits, as some say thugs wear prison stripes and sagging pants. Some reside within Crack Houses, while others reside, in homes of great opulence and grandeur, purchased through unscrupulous means. So, the definition of THUG lies within your perception. Both classifications of THUG possess common qualities, both are thugs of opportunity, and of chance. A THUG IS A THUG, IS A THUG, IS A THUG, it matters not the cosmetic makeup! All around the world, same song.

The practitioners of Criminal Justice, and stock holders of the lucrative Private Prison Corporations are making out like "bandits". Is there any wonder that this system goes under the moniker of "CRIMINAL"? In many instances, the system comes across as a criminal, criminal system. Crime may not pay as some have said, yet the Criminal Justice System, i.e., Bail bondsmen, Judges, Lawyers, etc., would seem to be in and on the Bear Market, of the Spectrum. So, we know the big dog profiteers of the system, and who remains to be their biggest commodity that keeps the machine grinding. A nation and a notion of supply and demand. CEO's and wealthy stock holders of the Private Prison Institutions are so greedy as to complain to State Legislators that particular jail occupancy rates are declining and aren't up to par, causing profiteers to seek legislation to reverse this trend. Now, who says CRIME DOESN'T PAY? These greedy "Smooth"(?) Criminals would beg to differ!

DIFFERENCES

If you aren't of the correct persuasion, for any perceived dubious and or diabolical occasion, be prepared for what will surely lead to litigation, and the possible likelihood of incarceration.

Only under the duress of natural and human directed disaster, has this nation found the gumption to display what is was founded to be; a nation, as one, under God! All I am saying in this book is, all that I desire is Life, Liberty, an equal opportunity, and the chance for pursuit of happiness for my children, grandchildren, and great grandchildren without the need for the existence of the AT LEAST, in a nation where their AT MOST should be guaranteed on an equal basis, socially, economically, and politically without a trace of BIAS. "Some say that I'm a Dreamer, but I'm not the only one"-The Beatles. It is as Rev. Al Sharpton so beautifully stated, "It's time for the Christian Right to start listening to the Right Christians"! This statement was made in reference to comments made by a club, two hundred and ninety-nine points short of Herman Cain's infamous 999 plan. Come to think of it, wasn't it the original Cain that

126

slew his Brother!? Our nation is sadly, and most assuredly eroding under the components of itself inflicted ACID.

(A)RROGANCE

(C)ONTEMPT

(I)NDIGNATION

(D)ENIAL

WHEN YOU LOOK AT THEM, WHAT DO YOU SEE? WHEN THEY LOOK AT YOU, WHAT DO THEY SEE?

Chapter 13
Prayerful Insight, Slanted Media

Clear, concise prayer leads to clear comprehensive thoughts, lead to clear positive conversation, lead to clear, life reviving, repentance...

When I can change my mind, I can change my world, When I can change my attitude, I can change my altitude, when I can educate, I can elevate.

This is the day the Lord has made, I will rejoice and be glad in it. It is time for the thoughts of my mind, heart, and soul to unite with pen and paper to give birth to the utterance of my being. Time to reveal, discuss, and possibly correct popular misconceptions. What happens when thoughts and deeds fail to correlate? "If you are who they thought you'd be, become who they thought you'd never be", stay within the realm of a Spiritual Dumb Ass (WHAT?), to gallop to realms unseen! Beware of the profit void of compassion, dog eat dog mentality!

Thank you, Lord, for Movies of the Spirit, such as Courageous, that inspire the mind, body, and Soul. Movies that remind one that "Time is truly of the essence", and as Baby Ruth would pray, "Lord turn us around, before it's everlasting too late. I Can Do ALL things, through Christ who strengthens me. (Phil 4:13) Dan and Dana Napier, to have surpassed the point of where "they" said you possibly could be, to the point of where "they" said you'd improbably never be, I salute you, in the words of the immortal Curtis Mayfield, "Keep on Pushing", Let there be Light!

Herman "Vain" Cain, the tea-party's main puppet stated, "America's being run by stupid people, I know, I counted them, and we outnumber the stupid people"(We're Dumber). Who is the "We", and what are their numbers, could it be nine hundred, and ninety-nine? Again Mr. Cain, you had to open your mouth, to the pleasure of the "We", not thinking of the implications, and applications that may offend, or amuse entire sections of the population, only to come across as a modern day "Rodchester", whatever you want me to say Mr. Benny!---In reference to comments made by Cain, were during the CPAC convention, 2/09/12.

"It was the best of times; it was the worst of times". It is a time to be fearful, it's a time to be faithful, it's a time of lack, a time of plenty, a time of joy, a time of pain, a time of wonder, a time of wonderment, a time of positivity, a time of doubt, a time when the wheat grows with the tare.

Life has never been so vivid, so lush, so precious, so greatly appreciated as when you have stared into the dark steely eyes of death!

Eccl. 9:11--time and chance happeneth to them all....

Currently examining the overt negative, and seemingly celebratory headlines by ESPN, almost hearing in frames of the da da da da da da, to paraphrase reframes from the "Wizard of Oz", ding dong the King is dead, the King is dead....C'mon man to lead with a headline stating "Mickelson schools Woods", what! Look over the total resumes of both golfer's work. Why are you attempting to barbeque, burn at the stake if you will, the one who has proven to be the cash-cow for the entire PGA. Would I be incorrect to perceive hints of racism that are clearly and slowly being unveiled? The ol' Gomer Pyle adage, I like him, but I don't love him, comes to mind. If Tiger were to not win another Major, he will undoubtedly still go down in history as one of the

Greatest Golfers of all time, if not the greatest. Does it rub you wrong that he happens to be Black, and has dominated a "white", game, sport, and field? Why could the headlines been more about Mickelson's come from behind victory, and less about Tiger's so-called meltdown. I'm sure Mickelson and Woods in the real world would appreciate proper coverage, and less tabloid B.S. Is Woods the bigger story in defeat, than Mickelson is in victory? An Atlanta Falcon Wide Receiver questions the validity of the continuing rising salary of the NFL Commissioner. I for one appreciate his machismo, in questioning "Master's" share of the revenue within the NFL. His assertion that the NFL would be nothing without the players is absolutely true. As one ESPN commentator stated, the players will come and go and no one would remember them after a few years, to some this may apply, yet it is also true of the Commissioners. No players, No games, No games, No revenue, No revenue, No League, No League, No Commissioner! Should the slave not question the master, and simply "lift that Bale, and tote that barge, shhh, nobody knows the trouble I've seen" Players whether you like it or not, you are simply the commodity of the team owners, and the commissioner who is supposed to be the pacifier (highest paid nipple) between player and owner is ruled by the highest bidder. Guess who that would be. True enough that the NFL is the highest grossing sports league in the world, yet where would it be if the commissioner hadn't any players? Ronnie White how dare you make eye contact and dare to speak to the MAN about his MANnerisms! How dare you, you ingrate!

I've had richness in my time, yet not to the point of excess. I've experienced poverty in my life, yet not of the overt variety. The main problem I've come to find in my life is being satisfied with mediocrity, and the notion of simply embracing the moniker of Human, when God created me to embrace the title of Human BEING! God made life to be in motion, change can only come through motion. At whatever so-called level of life one finds themselves, you will never achieve the next level through mediocrity, or standing still. Get up and go for what God intended for you. Celebrate the Human Being, as opposed to the Human Is-ing. As if to emphasize my point of a week ago, concerning negative reporting by ESPN, concerning Tiger Wood's so-called meltdown during the Pebble Beach Pro-Am. I curiously noticed there was an absence of headlines declaring a Meltdown by Phil Mickelson, during a three-way playoff at the Northern

Trust Open. Am I to be perceived as so naive as to not notice the difference in reporting when it come to some folks' biases. C'mon Man, is the field of Sports Journalism also slanted?!!?

1. WEAPONS of mass destruction

2. domestic abuse, rape, dog fighting, hypocritical selected uproars.

3. Hired, blinded by temporal success, goons who present a side that is only pleasing to certain segments of society(those they deem essential). Saying what they what they are instructed to say by those for the sake of political correctness, know that they can't say without consequences! i.e., You can take the Girl out of Compton, but you can't take the Compton out of the Girl! via, WW, how you doing?

4. Jared of subway fame exposed as a pedophile. His punishment is basically a slap on the wrist, yet over nine years later M. Vick is still vilified.

5. Symbicort, a medicine used for the treatment of COPD, a condition where enough oxygen can't be inhaled, or exhaled. What is the treatment for LDD, (Low Discernment Disorder).

AT LEAST I'M WHITE, IN THIS NATION (HE feels justified in being elated that HE ain't BLACK! I doubt if he could survive the Reality and Responsibility.

Ferguson, Mo.,

Judge, Jury, and Prevent the Executioner! How can a wolf (McMillon) in sheep's clothing preside as Prosecutor over the proceedings of a wolf (D, Wilson)? That is equivalent to the Klan prosecuting J. Earl Ray, or Huey Newton prosecuting the Panther Party! Eyes wide shut!

Why must Reality be so polar opposite than The Dream of Racial Harmony?

Finding Love in Hopeless Places.

To sit is a contented position, to be quiet is to sleep! Cry out!

134

"The only thing necessary for the triumph of evil is for good men to do nothing"-Edmund Burke(1729-1797)

Surviving a Mutable Nation through the Grace of an Immutable God! A nation whose strength is found in Lust, distancing itself from the Healing Power of Love. Thy will be done on Earth, as it is in Heaven!

A nation whose Cancer of Hate is seemingly in its Fourth Deadly Stage, metathesizing throughout the Land!

Slogans and Catch Phrases! Why is there a crack in the LIBERTY BELL? Could it be that its toll of equality rang untrue?

AFFLUENZA- A case for unjustified Justice of the Elite; the best Freedom money can buy. It is believed that AFFLUENZA is on the run, and has jumped bail, with supposed help from his mother! Say it ain't so!

IMSOPOENZA-unable to pay one's way to innocence.

How could one flee a Stiff necked, hard hearted elitist Kingdom, only to establish an elitist hardhearted, stiff necked nation?

Only those that claim that the BLACK LIVES MATTER movement has gotten out of hand, have themselves more than likely only seriously considered that their lives exclusively were the only lives that mattered and are worthy of consideration, maintaining their snobbish, let them eat cake, blasé, status quo approach to life. Because I'm speaking out on certain social issues, some will label me as anti-white! To the contrary, I'm only addressing issues of discrimination, racial injustice, and national differences, and indifferences within those realms. The paramount issue that would rank highly in my ANTI file would be that of ANTI-IGNORANCE, (IGNORANCE) which is the main component of hate and indifference.

This nation's history has always been to dispense, dispel, and incarcerate that which is misunderstood and feared, i.e., The Trail of Tears, The Dred Scott Case, Japanese American Internment, Afro-American Enslavement, etc., legacy of a Free Nation, only in America! "And Crown thy Good, with Brotherhood", Really, Really?

136

I'm not stating that I am of the opinion, that one segment of our society is exclusively to blame for our current state of affairs, I am, Truth be told, saying that one segment is at the root core of stated conditions.

Think about it, OPPORTUNITY DENIED, is OPPORTUNITY LOST! We must collectively rage against the current machine! "Ignorance is the Night of the Mind. A night without a moon or stars" - Confucions. For those who would fight against True Brotherhood of Mankind, it is not a question of equality, rather it is the fear of being surpassed, and of the reciprocity of what has been hatefully, selfishly, blindly Given. Righteous Indignation, while awaiting Righteous Reciprocity, and those fearful of the Karma within.

CONCLUSION

There will only be True Reckoning of a Nation, that, through the cleansing redemptive power of the Blood of Christ. Inviting the return of RIGHTEOUSNESS, a true RIGHTEOUSNESS falsely claimed at this Nation's inception. Those best fitted to acquire power are usually the least fitted to exercise said power. Tiring of being your Scapegoat, your Whipping Boy, your excuses for your frustration, your shortcomings, your Guilt! You, the AT LEAST, Pillars of Society! Jordan Davis, Trayvon Martin, Michael Brown, victimized by sociopathic At Least Minds. G. Zimmerman, twisted deprived soul, possessed of the Elitist Entitled Demons. Michael Dunn-eyes of the soul wide shut! To the Living, we owe respect. To the Dead, we owe the Truth!--

Voltaire

It matters not how fine the texture, nor the lay of the cloth that covers the ugliness of the heart, the true nature which lies within cannot forever be concealed and the truth shall be revealed! If you want to know the quality of a car's engine listen to its idling purr! Listen to an individual's conversation and it will reveal what is of one's character. For with the mouth, the contents of the Heart are Revealed. What does your Vrooooomm reveal about you? Are you the quite strong, engine of a Jaguar XJ6, or the backfiring muffler of a broken down hooptie?

JFMB - JUST FOR MY BROTHAS

To win the same race some merely have to stroll to win, I must be prepared to not only persevere, I MUST SPRINT with the mentality and perseverance of a Marathon Runner! IF you are disgusted by CRIMES OF PRIVILEGE, you just might be a member of a Minority within the U.S., and if you aren't disgusted there is a strong possibility you are a viable candidate for the AT LEAST I'M WHITE fan club.

Sports Illustrated Sportsperson of the Year, Serena Williams creates an uproar by those who feel that a Horse, a Horse, American Pharaoh, should have been awarded that (Person of the Year) Distinction! Really! Now is the time, where all good men must come to the aid of their fellowman. DIFFERENT Means, DIFFERENT Methods, SAME GAME (COMMERCE), DIFFERENT Outcomes. Forever be concealed, and the truth shall be revealed! What is done in the darkness of the Heart, must eventually be revealed through the light of truth.

The Journey to the completion of this book has been a tale of BROKENNESS. BROKENNESS that has served as a meaningful purpose of revelation. (Romans 8:28) The last three Presidential Nominations, and Elections have served to be the further unmasking and exposure of the naked truth of the Divisions that are far too prevalent, yet far too ignored within this Nation. Some of the so-called Great Minds of this Nation, particularly those of the prominent Media empire known as Radio and TV Talk Show Commentary, have been proven to possess Souls that dwell in the Sewers of Negativity. The names Beck, O'Reily, Limbaugh and Williams quickly come to mind when Negativity and particularly Racial Negativity is the subject being observed. I've learned along the way that brokenness is an essential component necessary if appreciation of a true miracle is to establish. Christ before His Greatest Miracles would always follow the order of Taking, Breaking, Blessing, and Using. Thank you, Lord, for always being right there during THE PROCESS!

Chapter 14
How Long, Odd Man Out, Unworthy

Yea though I walk through the valley of the shadow of death, I will fear no evil, for thou art with me....Surely goodness and mercy shall follow me all the days of my life. I really love the concept of being stalked and pursued by Goodness, and Mercy although life at times has me questioning, when will I be apprehended, and when will Grace and Mercy overtake me. I know I must remain humble, I must remain patient, I must envision what is before me. (Isa. 40:31) (2 Th 3:1-3) (Gal. 6:9) (Ps 30:5). Right now nation, I feel its morning time. Social unrest suggests its morning time, i.e., Occupy Wall Street Movement

Only when one acts, performs, lives, and adhere to standards of which you deem acceptable, will one be acknowledged, i.e., Halle Berry, (Monster's Ball), Denzel Washington, (Training Day), Herman Cain,(Aspiring Politician), i.e. and the list goes on. Only when we fit that role in the way you perceive, and therefore see us. Only when we stay in our so-called place, in our designated lane.

How dare one to speak his mind, or live their life as they deem fit, when that occurs we are demonized, and diminished, called uppity if you will, i.e., Terrell Owens, Muhammed Ali, Curt Flood, etc. of the sports entertainment field, Barack Obama, Colin Powell, etc., in the political field, Martin Luther King Jr., Shirley Chisolm, Rosa Parks, etc. in the social consciousness arena.

2 Ch 7:14 - If my people which are called by my name, would humble themselves and pray, and seek my face, and turn from their wicked ways then will I hear from heaven, and forgive their sin, and will heal their land...

*Dan. 5:26 -28 - Mene, Mene...*People read your word!

The Beatles had a song which said, "Come together right now over me", can you imagine the concept, and the tremendous outcome of such an event?--"He say I know you, you know me, one thing I can tell is you got to be free". If we, the world, would all come together, one faith, one hope, one God, one Belief, what a beautiful world it would be. Never be so enthralled with the external, that the blessings of the internal go astray.-----Closing Chapters

Tattoos-outward (permanent) expressions of internal (temporal) feelings.

Never allow the negative to out maneuver the positive. Live in the pluses.

The expediency of wrong, as right seemingly, is lethargic. Now, I have arrived at the point of urgency, the time to move past the envision, to that of fruition. To my Grandsons, nephews, and sons this book is for you. God has blessed me with beautiful, bright, and compassionate Daughters, Granddaughters, and nieces, and I'm sure they too will agree they also encounter the problems of race, blatant and passive. Heavenly Father give me the Strength, and the Grace, to see this thing through.

Now that I am in the third quarter of my life, the third life-mester if you will, I feel it is time for the birthing of this writing. Feel my push, hear my screen, this baby is on its way! So sad, most of my life had been lived in the twentieth century, and a vast amount of the same negativity that existed then, exists now in this the twenty first century where I will spend the rest of my life, and my children and grandchildren will spend the majority of their life. I'm writing this book as a lasting reminder, a lasting warning, and lasting encouragement. Had I known then, what I know now-- Appreciate the process--"I wouldn't give nothing for my journey"--Your latter days will be greater than your former days.--Encourage my grandson to learn the importance of perseverance, and positive pride motivated by positive stimulus, and to always learn from your mistakes. As much as possible make sure your words, and actions are God-inspired, whether consciously, or subconsciously. God's way automatically.

Let's see it (witness), let's hear it (slow to speak- prudent), let's read it, let's write it, let's right it for the Boys! "Our people perish for a lack of knowledge" (Has. 4:6) My heart sometimes aches for I know what is before them. I rejoice for I know who is for them, and the prosperity of body, and soul that awaits them. Discerning palatial palates seldom hunger (international), blind eyes rarely weep(observation).---Why would a hungry man crave what he's never had, that may be beyond his reach? How can a blind man (the well to do) observe what he refuses to see? (closes his eyes to). Know how to Hob nob with the worst of us, and the best of us.

NO SON, know sin, KNOW SON, no sin!

I have always used negativity to be my propellant toward a positive outcome. As my pastor frequently states, "Make your Haters your elevators". I am so shameful of the amount of time it has taken me to complete this assignment, so shameless my approach to the material covered. I must work the work of Him who sent me, while it is day, for the night comes that no man can work. I realize I am by no means a spring chicken, as well as the fact I don't quite have one foot in the grave that I'm aware of just yet. In hope of the diminishing the blows and number of disappointments my grandson will endure within his lifetime. Let him know how to roll with the punches if you see them coming, and make no doubt about it, they will be coming. Until now I have been shamelessly entertaining procrastination. Whether from shameless to shameful, no longer will procrastination dominate me. From this point on, and with my Heavenly Father's presence, I must complete my task for the Children. "Once a task is begun, never leave it until it is done", those words that my father often quoted to me still ring true today. Nourish, exercise, rest--A body at rest tends to stay at rest, a body and mind in motion will thus tend to stay in motion... Let not God given thought, dreams, and visions lay dormant. I must stay true to my task knowing that the "Steps of a righteous (Good) man are ordered by God"-- Paraphrased Psa.: 37:23

At my inconvenience, thank you Father for conveniently allowing me to share what you have revealed to me, what should be crystal clear even in these cloudy times. The truth subdued has been lacking the main ingredients for its flourishing, nurturing power. Lord, strengthen me in my task of pulling back the veils of hatred, bigotry, and negative thoughts and actions. If by chance, in the process, I have or will rub some shallow, and even deep-thinking individuals the wrong way, that is purely intentional. Whether you agree or disagree, I have encouraged you to think. Realize there is no repentance without a change of mind. It is my job to convince you, that the path to Peace of mind, and prosperity of the soul, whether carnal or spiritual is hidden in the disguise of mediocrity, and blatant stupidity. What happens after the Hip has Hopped, the Bling has Blang, and the game ain't hating anymore, because you've been played. Thank you, Lord, for using me as an abrasive, agitating, itchy, dumb ass.

Warning, somethin' is just around the bend--Been there, heard that, done that, felt that, got the tee-shirt, even though I don't want to go back, this side trip somehow always make itself part of the travel plans. The dangers of being Superficial--being at, on, or near the surface. Fake or artificial -- (Antonym--comprehensive, serious, thorough, deep. "Study to shew thyself approved"—2 Ti: 2:15. How selfish of me, when I realize how precious the gift! So much I know that you don't, so much you know that I don't. One may consider one mundane, and the other complex, yet what is one without the other? Can't we all get along! Grandma told me, "it's enough I don't know to create another world", face the facts. Hide and seek-hiding in broad daylight. some are even told where to hide (tax loopholes, off-shore bank accounts, i.e., legal cheating legislation). What is the color of success, does color determine success?

I've finally come to my place of No More. No More putting off tomorrow, for what should have been done yesterday, no more tolerating the intolerable, no more yes where there should have been no, no more holding back when I should be springing forth, no more bitterness where there should be love, no more mediocrity, where God has put excellence, no more settling, where there should be striving, no more vision, without fruition, no more getting, where there is no giving, no more black, where there is no red, brown, yellow, and white.(I need you, you need me, we're all a part of God's body). To be the proverbial, "Odd-man out, the last man chosen, to never leave the bench, to be the old toy in the bottom of box, only "played" with, when others show interest. To be underappreciated, and never needed, to have the position, and not the power. To be seen and not heard. Why aren't those people happy, why can't they be satisfied with what is? Why can't they trust us, to do it our way, the "white", oh I'm sorry, the right way!

"When the missionaries came to Africa, they had the Bible and we had the land. They said, "Let us Pray". We closed our eyes. When we opened them, we had the Bible, and they had the Land"--Bishop Desmond Tutu. And let the Native American Indians, say Amen!

Thanks to my Lord and Savior, Jesus Christ, for my assignments in life. No matter how large, or how small, whether I succeed, or I appear to fail, if I'm fat or I'm slim, whether I'm rich, or I'm poor, and especially if I'm white, green, purple, orange, or black. Thank you, Lord, for considering me, and guaranteeing the successful completion of the task at hand. My head, my heart, and my soul will be bloodied, along the way, yet never bowed. I must focus as Paul said, on the mark of the high calling! I'm in it to win it, detours, and stumbling blocks surely await in my path, but I must persevere. The cards dealt, were the cards meant. God promised he wouldn't put more on me than I, through Him could bear.

At least Judas applied a kiss, before he betrayed Christ!! It is extremely damaging, hurting, and dehumanizing, when one is betrayed by that which one once believed had valued, and loved them. As once sang, by Gloria Gaynor, with God's Love, "I WILL SURVIVE".

"Let's not rush to justice", "Let's not try this case in the court of public opinion", these are phrases often heard in high profile cases, especially cases involving the so-called "silent", majority, as the defendant. This nation if we are truthful with ourselves is a total antithesis of what it was supposedly founded upon. A nation of haves and have nots, where there is a vanishing," in between". A nation, where one segment is labeled as "Thugs", while the other is nothing more than "Misguided, and misunderstood". I live within a nation where I am judged every day, whether I am walking, jogging, driving, working, riding on an elevator, talking, and heaven forbid that I am held accountable for thinking, and expressing my thoughts, especially if those thoughts are contrary to your way of thinking. Isn't there a passage in the Bible, that states, "Judge not, lest ye be judged", (Matt.7:1, 2).

The quest to be "IN"cluded, in what has traditionally been an "EX"clusive, elitist, and overtly selfish nation of "Haves and Have-nots, with little room in between. We have always put on a great facade of being the nation of Great Opportunity for all that live therein. Yet, because of an elitist, "I've got mine, you get yours", mentality of exclusivity this nation is truly not living up to its creed, of liberty and justice for all. The haves more than not aren't willing to give a "Hand Up", rather viewing any government programs for the less fortunate, as "Hand Outs". The I've got mine, and I'm keeping all of mine, can only be termed as Selfish, Uncaring, Greed! Let us examine, the disgust some feel while viewing a young man, with his cap on sideways, baggy, sagging pants, with underwear in plain view, foul language without regard

150

to who is within range of hearing! Some are very quick to assume these young men are thugs, menaces to society, heading nowhere, and are of no societal redeeming value. Now let's view the born with a silver spoon, Polo wearing, BMW driving, best college attending, future pillars of our society, by way of Daddy's money, and are given society's thumbs up, society's second chances. Yet some things aren't always what they seem, can one say Jeffrey Domier, Ted Bundy, Charles Whitman, The Columbine Killers, Bernie Madoff, executives of Sachs-Goldman, etc. Let it not be interpreted that I am saying that all silver spoon, Polo wearing, BMW driving, best college attending, young men are all serial killers, or Ponzi Schemers, or market manipulators. I am saying that not all sagging pants, foul language spewing, and sideways cap donning, young men are Thugs. The difference here is outlook and opportunity. One is pretension, and the other can be attributed to perception. "So as a man believeth in his heart, so is He" (Prov. .23:7).

INcluded, INspired, INconsideration, EXcluded, EXpelled, EXcommunicated, IN-EXcessible, INexcusible!

I profess to be a simple man, with a simple observation, of a complicated society, in a complicated world, of complicated problems, within reach of a simple answer. It is of great importance that I complete my assignment in this observation, hopefully to eventually get to the simple answer to enable my children, grandchildren, and great-grandchildren the possibility of an abundant life. Internal strife, isolation, segregation, and classifications also lead to degradation, and sometimes loathing. All we need is Love-Beatles, Love's in need of Love-Stevie Wonder. The need for self-realization of who we truly are in and through Christ! In whatsoever state, I've learned to be content--Paul (Phil. 4:11). The childhood that we take into adulthood, and some aspects of that childhood that must be left behind. (II Tim: 2:22). We must learn to let go of what proves to be negative, as we mature chronologically, mentally, and spiritually. (I Cor. .13:11). Will we ever be as one? One Family of Man, one divided, or hopefully united. And the three, (The Father, Son, and Holy Spirit), are as one! He's too heavy, and he ain't my Brother! Overwhelming to think of the possibilities, the joy the peace possible of a Brotherhood of Man, a Brotherhood of equality, yet in what is now reality, what remains is your "At Least I'm White"! A guiltless, no repentant, pleasure which should be thoroughly reviewed, and extinguished.

To be taken for granted, and never embraced. Imagine the world, had we not taken Gandhi, King, Teresa, Kennedy, Malcom, all now gone, for granted. While we have time, embrace trumpeters of Love, Peace, justice and understanding, led by Jesus Christ, and others such as Angelou, Anderson, Jakes, Osteen, Dyer, Obama, and others who stand on a platform whose foundation is Love and forgiveness of the frailties(sins) of mankind, as commanded in the Holy Scriptures. "Love Ye one another, as you Love Yourself" (John 13:34). God made me who "I AM". Thank you for the realization, that I must be a Subjective being, that exists in an Objective World. God made us all to be prosperous, to be compassionate, and to be loving. If we could all pull our respective loads in the same direction, with the same goal in mind, with universal synchronicity, what a beautiful world it would be. "A house divided against itself... (Luke 11:17), (2 Cor. 6:14). Come on people, let's get together, now in unison, can we say, "When I move, you move just like that"! Whether scornfully ridiculed, or warmly embraced, whether read by one, or a million, I must subjectively complete my assignment. I must work the work of--(John 9:4). The light of Love must overpower the wickedness of Darkness. Love is all we need! I can no longer be fixin to, or fittin to, procrastination has been my nemesis far too long, it is time to complete this assignment. I am the victim, product, citizen, observer, and participant in an, "only if I have to", segregated, integrated society! Socially, economically, and politically. I was in high school during the great prevalence of the "I'm Black and I'm Proud, and the "Don't hate me, AT Least I'm White", regimes.

Unworthy of the treatment, nevertheless come on with the stones-"Have you considered my servant...?" The irony in writing this book is that what should be unnecessary has become of utmost necessity. This book is derived from the facts that there are alliable rights and needs within society that are not being properly and fairly instilled and distributed. There are glaring episodes in many lives, that are totally being ignored. Where there are assumptions void of consideration and thorough observation, there is virtually little or no deliberation in the form of correction which is in essence, i.e. bias and bigotry. There exist so many things in this United Nation that because of complacency and competitive fear that are remaining unattended to through true love and good for all brotherhood are long overdue, these things should have already taken place involuntarily and automatically. It should dwell within everyone's God-Given nature. On many occasions one will hear co-workers, clergy, politicians, family members, etc., state "I feel your pain! Really? If this were true why isn't anything being done aggressively to alleviate and finally eradicate the symptoms and realities of what is negative in another's existence as a rightful citizen of the United States of America, yet who is viewed and classified only as a Black (To some in the lowest connotation)Citizen. If you feel my pain, why are you fighting me, hindering me? Why can't you, why won't you do something!!

Please get the lesson of The Olive Tree. To harvest the Olive, its tree trunk must be shaken. To get the Olive's precious oil, the olive must be crushed. To obtain precipitation some condensation must take place. For them to increase, I must decrease.

In order to get the fruit of the Olive Tree, a machine is attached to the trunk of the tree with the sole purpose of shaking the fruit from its limbs. A net (safety) is placed at the base of the tree in order to make harvesting easier. Once harvested the process isn't over, the fruit must then go through a series of cleansing and crushing procedures to extract the precious ointment within the fruit. As it is in the natural, so it is also in the spiritual and vice versa. In order to experience the best of a person, a MACHINE is attached to the soul of that person for the lone purpose of shaking and separating the fruit of the spirit from every essence of being within that individual, and to separate the Wheat from the Chaff! "Our battle is not against flesh, and blood, but against powers and principalities....", yet the safety net in this case of this individual is rooted in the good soil which is Jesus Christ. Just as the Olive is crushed, so too must the individual be crushed in order to extract its ointment of anointment. "You meant it for my bad, but God meant it for my good..."!

The caged and cornered individual is left with no other alternative that to come out fighting in the role of the underdog who would be King. This may sound familiar to some, i.e. from the "Pit to the Palace," Let it Be! What happens when your past is better than your present, and your present, seems far greater than your future. Why shouldn't we all pray for the progress of a nation, rather than go back to a Greatness that wasn't shared by all?

To be a blow-heart, has been, that truly, probably in many thought and hearts is a never was, who incidentally rode to fame of his papa's coat tails it would behoove you Jr. to pull down your ten gallon hat over your head tightly and simply shut-up, especially when it comes to politics, and respect for the office of President of the United States, for you have truly achieved what some would consider physically impossible, You've allowed your quick lips to overload your over abundant ass. It would seem that you must be akin to that other blow-heart Bow and Arrow toting rocker. Now that your music careers, have been on a slippery slope to obscurity, you've now taken on the mantel of Stupid Has-beens, saviors of the race, whose only means of remaining in what is a dimming spot light, is to toss stones at the Glaring spotlight of others. Be slow to speak, and slow to anger. An old adage that would benefit you both, "It is better to keep your mouth shut, and allow folks to think you are a fool, than to open your mouth and remove all doubt". Are you ready for some......Reasoning? Timothy Olmstead--6th Grade Teacher at the Heights Community School in St. Paul, Mn. voluntarily

157

resigned. He told the entire class that is easier for him to teach rich White folks than poor Black people.

You felt you had buried me, only to realize you had only planted me. In order for a seed to germinate, it must experience the planting, the solitude, the darkness. Properly nourished, and cultivated, I will eventually reach my ultimate potential, and being. In reference to the sixth-grade teacher who would resign rather than teach poor black kids, it is a poor observation into your dedication to the profession of teaching, rich or poor, and to your qualities of being a God fearing, Human being loving, decent Human Being. Could it be that you were void of the skills and preparation necessary to be a teacher that would bring pride to the profession. Were you not up to the task? What was really going on. Just be a man about it! Still some enquiring minds want to know; How do we meet the challenge of a divided United Nation, where do we go from here?

Finish It:

As I neared the completion of this book, it occurred to me, what would be the impetus to convince one to complete the reading of this book. To convince one to read further than the first few paragraphs there must exist some thoughts, interesting and intriguing to the point of further exploration. Yet, to get it read at all, I must finish. To finish strong, an explosive start must be attained out of the blocks. Its time is NOW, no more excuses, no more waiting, so, hold on, here we go. Thank you, Lord, for trusting me with this assignment, knowing within Your Will it would get done within your timing, through your guidance, wisdom, and instruction. As my Grandmother would often sing, so too am I within my Spirit, "When I'm on my mission Lord, won't you guide me, oh, teach me how to watch, fight, and pray". I too have found out, "If I trust HIM, HE will Provide".

There are so many life episodes within my psyche, whose time for revelation is NOW. Whether those instances be interesting, and/or be write worthy, I believe them to be so, and should be shared. The Negative within the camera will not produce a photograph if the Negative is not exposed to the Light. This will be a book dealing with this Nation's dealings with Race Relations and its affect it has on its people situationally, economically, politically, socially, and morally. From my point of view this Nation, no matter how pretty the picture it attempts to display to the rest

159

of the Universe, is singing an old Blues tune by Bobby Blue Bland, that I will paraphrase, "Ain't no Love in the HEART of the Nation, ain't no love in the heart of the city, ain't no love, and ain't it a pity, ain't no Love in the Heart of the Nation". We are living in a Nation, and a notion where the government, and its people are seemingly living a life of Bipolar tendencies.

BIPOLAR: (adj) having or relating to two poles or extremities. A.) also known as manic depression, is a mental (spiritual, moral) illness that brings severe high and low moods and changes in sleep, energy, thinking, and behavior.

To be affected nationally with symptoms is to suggest that we are living in a Nation Divided with very little in COMMON, each at opposite ends of the pole. For the life of me it is sometimes difficult for me to rectify the necessity and to what degree this book should be written. My story may very well not be your story, yet this story and others of the same nature has happened, is happening and from the looks of current affairs and events which lead to the assumption and evidence of the direction and conscience of this

Nation. This story is too real, and too often the somewhat never-ending saga, whose happily ever after isn't guaranteed, and whose ending depends on which side of the fence your compassion, and your moral compass or lack thereof hangs their hat.

Ironically for the very reasons I shouldn't find it necessary to write this book, are the very factors that are insistent that I must.

Consider yourself privileged to partake of a part of me that screams to be shared. Take a firm grip of the drawstrings that pull back the curtains of reality to reveal with transparency of the "lies" of fake realities, allegiances, and brotherhoods of a nation of Liberty and Justice for all. To have mastered the art of the "LIE" as to manipulate a convenient "TRUTH" grounded in "Falsehoods". To perceive Greatness for one, and to neglect another is Fake prosperity. To make any circumstance Great Again, suggests that at one time Greatness existed. (If the circumstances aren't Great for all, are those Circumstances Great for any?)

To write of a Nation and a Notion where one man's beautiful reality in any part is at the expense of another man's horrendous nightmare especially in the realm of Racial Harmony and Equality, should be a nonfactor, yet here we are.

Some will recognize, some will deny, and pitifully some have lived within a bubble of exclusivity and privilege as to deny the relevance of this book, yet, write I must. One can't clear (life's) hurdles until one first sheds one's warmups, completed stretching, gets in the blocks, and once the starter's gun fires signifying the start, then quickly and aggressively approach said hurdles, clear the hurdles in anticipation to compete well and then "Finish" the race.

Thinkers, pro and con, the time of stretching, and loosening up, and shedding warm-up apparel is upon us. It is now time to take your (BOOK) marks to proceed with our thoughts and ideas and revelations on RACE. Give me your tired, your poor, your huddled masses, yearning to be free. The wretched refuse of your teeming shore. Send these, the homeless, tempest tossed to me, I lift my Lamp beside the golden door. Emma Lazarus-- Inscription of the Statue of Liberty. How far have we been removed from those sentiments, or were they ever sincerely meant?

Chapter 15
HENCE, THEREFORE, NEVERTHELESS

An American Society Cultural Attitude prevalent in the mindset of those who mistakenly have been misled to feel privileged to possess the blessing (?) of AT LEAST I'M WHITE.

HENCE, THEREFORE, NEVERTHELESS

1 Corinthians 13:2 (NIV)-If I speak in the tongues of men or of angels, but do not have love, I am only a resounding gong or a clanging cymbal.

Talking loud and saying nothing, talking out the side of your neck, etc.

1 Corinthians 13:2 (KJV) -Though I speak with the tongues of men and of angels, and have not charity, I am become as sounding brass, or a tinkling cymbal.

Isaiah 1:18 (KJV) – Come now and let us reason together, saith the Lord: though your sins be as scarlet, they shall be as white as snow; though they be red like crimson, they shall be as wool.

PSALM 133:1 (NIV) - How good and pleasant it is when God's people live together in unity!

These scriptures speak of unity, warn of deception, and of solution to this nation's divisions, especially along racial lines. So sad, that too many have taken on the unfeeling, mantra of the ignorant privileged elite; HENCE, THEREFORE, NEVERTHELESS WHAT WAS SAID, WHAT WAS HEARD HENCE, THEREFORE, NEVERTHELESS

HENCE (adv)-1. for this reason, 2. for this reason, my mind is made up.

THEREFORE (adv) -1. for that reason, consequently. "It has been proven to be".

NEVERTHELESS (adv)-In spite of that, notwithstanding, all the same.

I owe you no explanation, nor consideration, due to the fact, "At Least I'm White"! A nation, any nation whose soul is found to be void of empathy and compassion for any segment of its culture and society renders its lofty words and ideals meaningless to all

164

society, whether those ideals be for "Liberty and Justice for All" or "Crowning thy good with Brotherhood". Such traits cause one to wonder why the Liberty Bell is cracked. Could it be that Liberty didn't ring true then as it doesn't today for all, and that the Bell's toll distanced itself from hypocrisy, upon which LIBERTY was established? Pray for any nation, where LIBERTY has been or is on trial. HIStory often gets sidetracked from the REALstory. Be Blessed as we attempt to move forward (with)empathy and compassion for all, distancing itself from the selfish mantras of "AT LEAST"!

ABSURD (adj)-wildly illogical or inappropriate (absurdity)

ABJECT (adj)-miserable, wretched, absolute and humiliating, self-abasing

ABASE (v)-humiliate or degrade

Consider with me, if you will the mindset and heart set of far too many who have the audacity to possess an abject absurdity that they feel legitimizes their "god" given right to abase who and what they feel to

165

be inferior to their birthright superiority, perceived to be by nature. Consider, too, that there is paradox in the validity within the confession and proclamation of the "At Least". Paradox, that what one proclaims to be their LEAST human quality is what has proven to be in this society your GREATEST asset in civil, social, economic, and political realms proven through actions derivative of a nation's heart, and mindset.

DERELICTION (n)-neglect, failure to carry out obligation, abandoning, being abandoned

DERIVE (v)-get, obtain, or form 2. Arrive from, originate in, be descended or obtained from

The value of being a Citizen of the United States, in the eyes of the world is quickly depreciating, when statements such as "at least I'm white" are used to diminish the status of others not of the same ilk and is being used as a mantra of pride in a nation supposed a melting pot, united in liberty and justice. Could it be that such tactics, and phrases and thinking is the answer and grounds upon which divisionary tactics are formed?

HATE (v)-feel intense dislike for or aversion to

FEAR (n)-panic or distress caused by exposure to danger, expectation of pain, etc.

This book has been written to explore, expose, and hopefully lead to rectification in some small way of the wrong that permeates the heart and mindsets cultivated by negative seeds planted in what should be fertile soil, that has now sprouted either hate and or fear that is masqueraded as Racial Pride and false superiority. If one possesses and is proud of a mantra that brags that their weakest quality, their at least, is somehow their greatest quality in comparison of human value, that person possesses what one rock singer once sang; A total Eclipse of the Heart.

LOVE (n)- deep affection; fondness

The answer, the cure to any of our perceived "At Least" is simply and overdose of what should be our "At Most", and that would be and should be LOVE! To those who would still proclaim with the vim and vigor displayed by the Cowardly Lion of the Wizard of Oz, that proudly boasted, "If I were King of the Forest,

167

your claim of "At Least I'm White', carries the same empty pitiful weight as the Lion's claim, which in a nation of Liberty and Justice for all should be of non-importance, and consequence. Yet, just as the foursome, on their trek to Oz, this nation, also is in search of courage, a brain, and a heart for ALL of its People. We too, as the foursome should discover what we are searching for and in need of, we've had all along. The sooner we all discover the values upon which this nation is founded, the sooner we will find that there truly is, "No place like Home"! I appeal to you, brothers and sisters, in the name of our Lord Jesus Christ, that all of you agree with one another in what you say, and that there be no divisions among you, but that you be perfectly united in mind and thought--1 Corinthians 1:10

A new commandment I give unto you, that ye Love one another, as I have loved you, that ye also Love one another - John 13:34

Greater Love hath no man than this, that a man lay down his life for his friends - John 15:13

168

SELFISHNESS and SACRIFICE cannot and will not coexist in a land of ALL. WE MUST allow LOVE of ALL MANKIND to be the VICTOR!

AT LEAST, be Blessed, AT LEAST, be a BLESSING, AT LEAST, be of MUCH LOVE!! GGT!

Chapter 16
Pol(tricks)

As with any disease of epic proportions, there will exist no semblance of a cure, until the symptoms are properly diagnosed, addressed, and hopefully successfully medicated, and eradicated. The problems within the racial interactions of this nation seemingly can be attributed to either an overabundance, or general lack thereof of four major factors, i.e., EDUCATION, EDIFICATION, ECONOMICS, and EGOS. Although we view life through different eyes, and from different cultural viewpoints, our common denominator that is striving to unite us, remains that of GENUINE LOVE of GOD and MANKIND.

Please, we must come to the conclusion sooner, rather than later of the fact that, I need you, you need me, we're all a part of God's body! It is His will that every need be supplied, you are important to me, I need you to survive! A beautiful refrain from a lovely song celebrating unity. Let's just face it, WE ARE ONE. DIFFERENCES shouldn't be meant as means to divide, rather differences should be celebrated, examined, and used toward the elation of diversity, and the God given ability to act as the various, spices of life. One's gifts that are unique to that one, should not be celebrated any more than those of others . Rather, we are all various pieces of a Life puzzle that fit in perfectly to create a lovely landscape! How can I help you, how can you help me to get to the destination, God desires that WE all to reach?

Thank you, Rev. Samuel Rodriguez for your admonition and reminder that, it's time to move, and to act quickly", the night isn't upon us yet, but the shadows are looming large, and that there exists a thin line between pathetic, and prophetic. Billy Preston sang a song that contained the lyrics, "will it go 'round in circles, or will it fly high like a bird up in the sky?" It is past time for the breaking of unfruitful cycles! When we can change our minds, we can change our world, when we can change our attitude, we'll change our altitude, and when we can educate, we will surely elevate. We must get out of these cycles that hold our nation, and our people in grips of perpetual negativity.

My people perish for a lack of knowledge - Hosea 4:6

As a rainbow coalition of people, we must all come to the realization that, we are all, chosen to be challenged, challenged to be blessed, and blessed to be

171

chosen. All things work toward the good...Romans 8:28

There is a way that seems right unto man, yet the end thereof leads to destruction - Proverbs 16:25

Beware of any quick fix, get rich schemes and solutions that are at the expense of any segment of society, justified by calling and deeming that segment, "Social, collateral damage.

Enter ye in at the strait gate, for wide is the way that leadeth to destruction, and many there be which go in there at....Matthew 7:13

Must it be necessary that evil snarls its hideous face, before "True Love" is manifested and activated?

For wherever Christ builds a Church, the devil builds a Temple----Martin Luther

I can only imagine if we were to all Love Now.

NOW - Now faith is the substance--Heb. 11:1

IF-If my people which are called by my name 2 Chron. 7:14

YE- Ye are the salt of the earth--Matt: 5:13

LET-Let this mind be in ye--Phil. 2:5

LOVE-Love ye, one another--John 15:12

My brothers and sisters, I truly pray for that day when the United States of America, truly becomes one Nation, Indivisible, under ONE GOD. A nation where all are granted the opportunity to attain their "AT MOST" far removed from the excuses of the "AT LEAST"! Some will ask, what is the answer, what is the solution.
MANY DIFFERENCES yet in need of ONE LOVE!

Think about this; there is a big difference between All One, and Alone. As it is with this nation, if true unity isn't found within All of our Hearts, and any one segment is ignored, and denied, AL(L) ONE, will find itself A(L)ONE in a nation that is supposedly built on the platform of Liberty and Justice for ALL! So very sad to have to admit, in spite of what we want to portray to the world, this nation has not progressed as much as it proclaims in the areas of civility, and human kindness. We thought, we had turned the

173

corner, so why so-many U-Turns? Does it really matter the hue of one's skin, if that person can adequately steer the ship of progress, without its opposing occupants continually punching holes in the vessel of progress. Will the "Dream", perpetually, simply be a dream to those who aspire for a better life? For those satisfied with your state of (UN)consciousness of selfishness, you may not be dreaming, yet you need to "WAKE-UP", from the Nightmares of your own making! I need you, and you need ME!

Political Conventions-Retreats of "feel good", back slapping, back stabbing, you rub my back, and I'll rub yours, grown-(down)up hypocrisy intended to increase efforts to bring the nation together through so-called positive efforts that cast us further apart, by means of separation. But, then "who cares", as long as I get my way, my agenda, and get my country back! Back to what? Back to what it was, on the brink of a fall, far from the foundation this nation was founded upon. Yet, that would be okay as long as it is my party holding the reins, when the wagons take the plunge over the cliffs of desperation. A grown-up conference, being played with Kid's Playground Standards; It's my ball, so we'll play by my rules, no add-ons, no changes! My Ball, My Game, My Rules, comprende',

Si or No? That little part is for our Bilingual delegates to welcome you, and for you to know we are an inclusive," exclusive", party!

I've eaten crumbs from the master's table, and I have faithfully gleaned behind the Reapers! It's now my turn at the Big Table, to be a legitimate part of and enjoy the fruits of the harvest. AT MOST, I'm a child of the King of Kings, which in many ways TRUMPS the best of your AT LEAST!

Come on man!!!! Two thirds of the Negro Race are brainwashed (when it comes to politics)? This after you've been referred to as the "Flavor of the Month", by the stalwart of the Tea Party, S. Palin. Let's take a stab shall we at Rocky Road, Chocolate, Nutty, with soft bits of White Marshmallow, that would seem more fitting. To think you took the FOTM statement as a compliment is beyond me. For you to make the two thirds reference was ludicrous and blatantly racist. We're you so blinded by your arrogant 999 plans, that you became ignorant to the fact that you were being used as a mouthpiece to say for them what could be considered socially, and politically incorrect, possibly leading to a moral, and deadly, self-inflicted, Throat Cutting of their Societal and Political aspirations. Come on Mr. H. Vain, after the Ballot Controversy of a state's straw poll victory, I bet you thought the song was about you! Come on Man! Had your 999 plans been flipped by little voices in your head to resemble the 666 plans, or is it the voice that is whispering to you, one of the two thirds sect, that can't be trusted to think for one's self? "No more backwards thinking, time for thinking ahead" so sang Harold Melvin and the Blue Notes. Yet you at the cost of political expediency made such an uncalled-for callous statement. Were you so easily baited by the Media? Will the remaining one third, that is by your assessment be capable level-headed reasoning and thinking, really want a leader who without thinking (you couldn't have been)so easily condemn a nearly entire race of people of being unable to intelligently participate in the American Way of Life? Of what percentile did you rank yourself? You sounded to be of the elitist persuasion, you know the one that states, "I've got mine, let them(I would assume the other two thirds) get theirs, ill, ilk"! Most young "thinking" non-brainwashed brothers and sisters would quite righteously, and politely refer to you as a modern, old school "Uncle Tom", seemingly has been used unawares by the system, or would you have wanted to be referred to as Uncle Tim. Did you really, after your references of the Afro American's power of

176

thought or lack thereof, really think that you could garner fifty percent or even two thirds of their votes in a dog fight, let alone a national political election? To further review how you were assessed by your own party, S. Palin was quoted as saying in reference to you that (He)"Doesn't look like he's part of that permanent political class"! Wow, Come on Man!! Come on now Mr. Man, the bible states in Isa. 1:18-- Come now and let us reason together. How could you so blatantly label an entire race of people of which you are a part without at least conferring with them (or was it in your opinion, that you had risen above them) or have you taken on the trait of the original Cain, who curiously asked of God, "Am I, my Brother's Keeper"? At a time when we should be seeking means of uniting mankind, we instead find ourselves pointing accusing damning fingers at one another. "Oh, it ain't my fault"! Herman as in Monster, Cain as in Brother Killer, equals Monster, Brother Killer. Your opinions can either edify you, or demonize you, therefore it would behoove and benefit us all to be slow to anger, and above all be slow to speak. Be sure of the facts Jack. As my grandmother, Baby Ruth Winn, would always say, "Speak what you know, and not before". Prov. 16:32--He that is slow to anger, is better than the mighty, and he that ruleth his spirit than he that taketh a city. (straw poll, primary, nation) Pick up the book, and take a look, better yet, heed. Talk about the pot calling the kettle black, Mr. Cain accuses R. Perry of being insensitive to Black People, because of a camp compound associated with the Perry Family supposedly named "Niggerhead". Well Mr. Vain, that fact may have been true, but at least according to reports, Mr. Perry did try to put a lid on his pot, while yours was still simmering with your "two thirds" statement, in plain view but true to your party's political antics. You have remained true to the script, by pointing the finger of blame in the opposite direction of self to defray attention away from your stewing mess, or did you not think that the one third wouldn't notice. The aroma of emanating from your mess left a lot to be desired, and possibly ignited a not so pleasant gag reflex.

If the rescuing of this Nation were dependent upon a Life Raft built upon your empathy, your understanding of the political machine and God forbid, that which you held most dear, your Money, well we would have known collectively in the words of song by Mary J. Blige, "I'm(we're) going Down"! What would happen if for thirty seconds the whole world could focus on something other than self, and for the edification of the brotherhood of mankind? Now to show how great(?) minds flow, we had Hank Williams Jr., virtually issuing Mr. Vain, a guaranteed kiss of political aspirations death, by endorsing him as his likely candidate of choice for the GOP's Presidential Nomination. A surer path for Mr. Vain, would have been to have Obama weigh in on the nominee and say that Mr. Vain would not be his likely choice, almost certainly the GOP would without a doubt, thought, or consideration, would have most assuredly guaranteed Mr. Vain, the nomination. Besides, who is H. Williams Jr., other than another ALIW, over the hill, crooner, living on his daddy's legacy. Again Mr. Williams, a word of advice my grandmother passed along; "It's better to keep your mouth shut, and allow folks to think you're a fool, then to open your mouth, and remove all doubt"!

Mr. Vain, The Iceman Cometh!

Waskily wabbit,(tricks are for kids), fly in the ointment, pain in the ass, thorn in my flesh, pesky gnat, ants at the picnic, etc., all terms to describe, the negro who is finally claiming a seat at the Grown-ups(?), table. Some feel that they possibly had slipped up, messed up, and banged up during the last presidential election. So now they are defiantly stating with bravado, "we're taking our nation back"! and never again. Then to my surprise, up pops the devil(?)with his Inverted "666" plan, He's tied with the party's nominee favorite for the popular vote survey poll, but lagging in the electability survey poll, and he's dare I say it a Black Man, who doesn't stand a snowball's chance in hell of obtaining the Republican party's Nomination as President of the United States. (Master likes it when the help put on a good fight, for their entertainment, house nigger mentality vs. field nigger mentality) It is amusing just to hear the GOP wheels turning in thought, we've been there (Have a Black President), done that, got the tee shirt, and don't ever want to go back again. And then couldn't you just imagine if both candidates running for President were Black, as one newspaper columnist stated the overwhelming sells for the vendor selling the T-Shirts for the 2012 election that states, "I'm Voting for the Black Guy"! Come on Mr. Vain, it's been fun, you've been used, thanks for the memories, but C'mon Man, you're so Cain, I bet you thought the "SONG", was about you! Did you really get into the mindset of

ALIW? then again maybe you are, because you most assuredly aren't a member of the two-thirds "brainwashed" sect, yet you truly come across as a Platinum, card carrying member of the white-washed sect.

Incredulous, Indignation

After viewing excerpts from the 10/18/11 Las Vegas GOP Debate, my principle thought that emerged was, can one imagine the incredulous, indignation that should be felt once the Bait's (HC), eyes are open to the fact, that he indeed has been baited,(used to be a semi-reasonable-facsimile, to say things to the so-called two-thirds, that the main components of the GOP want to, yet know they can't, if they are to have any semblance of luring(bait), the minority vote, the player has been played, and the jig is up. As Rick Perry stated, I Love You Herman, but BROTHER! C'mon man, he just hit you with a T-party's version of Nigger Please! As George Benson sang and asked so beautifully, Mr. Vain, are you, "Lost in a Masquerade?" Let's look shall we at the United States of TNA, Tendencies, Nature, and Attitude. The word states in Prov. 23:7, as a man thinketh in his

181

heart, so is he - Attitude. If one possesses the attitude of an Elitist, his nature and tendencies are that of a selfish, me and only me, I've got mine, whether you get yours or not, is purely not of my concern, which is very close to the answer given by Cain, when asked by God, where was his brother Abel, "Am I my brother's keeper"?

Francis of Asisi once wrote - Lord make me an instrument of your Praise

Past Due, The Ministry of a Dumb-Ass— "Recoverme". God and Country-a country built on these two principles-From My Country 'tis of Thee, to My Country 'tis of "D"--Believing that your prosperity is based on "Me", rather than "THEE". Thank you, Dr. Cindy Trimm, that during the 2011 Woman thou art loosed, conference, you reminded me that I as a man who was deliberately eavesdropping, that I too, come Loaded with what God has equipped me with, and it is time for me to push, the wait is over! The Higher the Heights, the deeper the depths, the lower the lows, the higher the aspirations! What happens when the elite of the elite, encounter the poor of the poor? To whom much is given, much is required(Luke 12:48) The humbler the beginnings, the sweeter the reward, as

182

Deaconess Carolyn Caldwell admonishes in her teachings during various speaking engagements," we've got to stay in the fight, at times while being propped up on every leaning side, yet it is important to stay low! There is leverage in lowliness!" Let no man think more highly of himself than he should (Rom: .12:3). There is much that can be said of and learned of the importance of that of one who has resigned to humility and fact of that of the "Spiritual Dumbass"(Num: .22:23).

The Tea Party's flavor of the month, Mr. Cain, is continually proving himself to be more of the MD 20/20, variety than that of Dom Perion, in other words, the party should not have served "No wine before its time", in other words you've been good for a quick buzz, but as for lasting savor upon the palate, it would seem you leave a lot to be desired, but as the saying goes, "You get what you pay for", and right now, you wouldn't be bought at a going out of business, fire sale. How Long Has This Been Going ON?--Ace, Van Morrison. How ridiculous--The Characters Elmo (Voice is that of a Black Man (Kevin Clash, exposed by the "View"), The man originally costumed as Barney, a Black Man. Devon LaRussa tweets Ron Washington is a crackhead! "I saw a crackhead doing the "Wash", today, coincidence? I think not.....It's a phrase I use, meant as a joke, please don't be offended!....Young Lady, when you're living in a glass house, please think before casting stones, i.e., your Dad's DUI conviction(s). Everyday there's somethin' new, that keeps me questioning you.

Ignorance of the entitled, equates to satisfaction of the mundane (mediocre). Our people perish (are destroyed) for a lack of knowledge—Has: 4:6. Bishop Jakes, I'm tired of being tired, it's time for the hunt(Manpower 2011, Breaking new ground), this Loin is about to roar, and my spirit is "Standing up to it". Tired of Giving in the absence of non-reciprocation, Tired of a government of selfish manipulation.

TIRED OF THE PUSH WHERE THERE IS NO PULL

Tired of The Push where there is no pull

never tire of Love

Tired of the Hate, where there is no cause

never tire of Love

Tired of the Lack of compassion, where there is a worthy cause

never tire of Love

Tired of the lack of Godly characteristics in a nation founded of love shaped with heavenly gloves, yet I'll never, never, never tire of Love

A Kiss, A hug, a touch, a care, tell me of one who wouldn't venture to dare

Never tire of Love.

HAVE A HEART

Have a Heart to give more than you may receive

Have a Heart that dares to care, never wary of the resultant stare

Have a Heart that places hate asunder, no matter the pressure one comes under.

Have a Heart using Christ as the Example, soon negativity it will trample

So as a man thinketh, so is he; Think Love, and its benefits, the better the world to be.

Have a Heart for Love, sent purely from above, have a heart for Love, Love, Love.

Burl Ives once sang a song titled "A Little Bitty Tear "with lyrics that said, "A little bitty tear let me down, spoiled my act as a clown, I had it made up not to make a frown, but a little bitty tear let me down." Now let's imagine what one potentially prominent triple nine, politician, may be singing these days, after possibly being proven guilty of sexual harassment--- (The beat goes on, John Edwards, T. Kennedy, J. Weiner, etc...) A little bitty (You fill in the blank), smear let me down, spoiled my act(?), as a clown, (Keep a stiff upper-lip), my mind was made up, (I don't know which part, the two-thirds brainwashed, or in this case the one-third, thinking sector) not to make a frown, but a little bitty smear let me down! Pizza-Pizza!--Can't buy me Love!

Headline--Cain blames Perry for smear! Don't hate the playa, hate the game. The game devised by the Non-Brainwashed, how ya like me now? As Stuts, and

Pretty Boy refers to him as the "Hermanator", of 999 acclaim, or in German, the "No-No-No", acclaim. AND THEN HE OPENED HIS MOUTH---RICK PERRY, AND HERMAN CAIN. One that is by all accounts within this society, an elitist, and the other who has been, pardon the reference, "Brainwashed", to think that he is in the same category, Again, "Can't buy me Love!", Mr. Vain "the nit-pickiness of the media"-------"when people get on the Cain train, they don't get off."

Luke 14:28--Count the cost--Be very careful to not take on other's attributes of "At Least", strive to make sure you are, at least, beginnings will have an at most ending.

Chapter 17
Necessary Outrage

There exists an urgency and relevancy within the Womb of NOW, that must be lying dormant in the wombs of the blasé, who couldn't care less for any LIVES MOVEMENT, other than their own.

The concept of #ALL LIVES (MATTER) sounds ideal, yet it has proven to be in this nation, that the mantra should read #ALL LIVES MATTER FOR SOME, and the eloquent notions and ideals written in the notable 1776 document were written for some, and definitely not for ALL, and because of the urgency of NOW it has become a lofty concept whose time and proclamation of Life, Liberty, and Freedom to pursue happiness is definitely NOW! So now, that NOW has our attention NOW, let us examine the auspices of why the importance of NOW, #BLACK LIVES MATTER. Open the eyes of our minds, body, and soul to the truth that #ALL LIVES (DON'T) MATTER, for and to far too many. Had the focus all along truly been ALL, the necessity for the cry of relevancy would be unnecessary. Could it be possible that the BETTER are now BITTER, that the BITTER are BETTER? LET

MY PEOPLE GO! Has Pharaoh, (the powers that be) become alarmed that the children of God are awakening and coming UP out of Egypt (a state of mind), that prompts the Pharaoh's to proclaim, "We're taking our Country back" and "Make America Great AGAIN"!

II Chronicles 14:7 reads as follows: If my people, which are called by my name, shall humble themselves, and pray, and seek my face, and turn from their wicked way; then will I hear from heaven, and forgive their sin, and will heal their land.

We proclaim to be a Christian Nation, yet we are not praying, and we definitely have an enormous problem with HUMILITY!

Had #ALL LIVES MATTER were an honest statement, where would the need for #BLACK LIVES MATTER, and #BLUE LIVES MATTER stakes their claim? Should it come as a surprise, that those who for years were Setting the Table, Building the Table, and Cleaning the Table, to then being denied a seat at the table, are now rightfully demanding their legitimate right to have a prominent seat at the "Grown-ups" table. For hundreds of years, existing only to be seen

189

and not heard, to being considered property and less than a fellow Human Being. Once emancipated from Human Bondage and Slavery, to only step into Legal Institutionalized Human and Mortal Bondage, a form of exclusive slavery. Having been subject to the do as I say and not as I do, one would not question why this sect of Humanity has a strong case to be BITTER, which leads one to wonder, why question and be in opposition to #BLACK LIVES MATTER.

This situation didn't really matter until said situation, began to knock on Comforts Door, and as a consequence the need for #ALL LIVES MATTER, and #BLUE LIVES MATTER, felt the need of relevancy. From the very inception of this country the Lives of Some was all that mattered, to the exclusion of those deemed unworthy of the same recognition. It is written in the Declaration of Independence that some were considered less than one hundred per cent human. It was further emphasized with the history of forced labor, whips, chains, lynching's, etc. Yes, some will argue that these are incidents of the past, yet I beg to differ. How can one proclaim defiantly that #ALL LIVES MATTER, to the exclusion of those who have (in many cases) innocently fallen victim to a Service Revolver that has replaced the Hangman's Noose, to those imprisoned for longer terms than those of a particular persuasion who have committed identical crimes?

PURPOSE: SIMPLE YET COMPLEX

To, Educate, Eradicate, and Elevate.

Psalm 139: 14 - I will praise Thee, for I am fearfully, and wonderfully made; marvelous are thy works, and that my soul knoweth right well.

ONLY LOVE CAN CONQUER HATE

James 5:1-10

1) GO to now, ye rich men, weep and howl for your miseries that shall come upon you.

2) Your riches are corrupted, and your garments are motheaten.

3) Your gold and silver are cankered; and the rust of them shall be a witness against you and shall eat your flesh as it were fire. Ye have heaped treasure together for the last days.

4) Behold, the hire of the laborer's who have reaped down your fields, which is of you kept back by fraud, crieth: and the cries of them which have reaped are entered into the ears of the Lord of sabaoth.

5) Ye have lived in pleasure on the earth, and been wanton; ye have nourished your hearts, as in a day of slaughter.

6) Ye have killed the just; and he doth not resist you.

7) Be patient therefore, brethren, unto the coming of the Lord. Behold, the husbandman waiteth for the precious fruit of the earth, and hath long patience for it, until he receives the early and latter rain.

8) Behold we count them happy which endure. Ye have heard of the patience of Job and have seen the end of the Lord: that the Lord is very pitiful, and of tender mercy.

9) But above all things, my brethren, swear not, neither by heaven, neither by the earth, neither by any other oath: But let your yea be yea; and your nay, nay; lest ye fall into condemnation.

10) Confess your faults one to another, and pray one for another, that ye may be healed. The effectual fervent prayer of a righteous man availeth much.

THE FEAR OF DREAM'S fruition AND REALITY'S CRUMBLING:

THE NECESSARY UNNECESSARY IF

AS I NEAR THE COMPLETION of this book, it is with sorrow and trepidation that I cannot complete this assignment without addressing the Elephant in the room of this nation's conscience known as #ALL LIVES MATTER. True, #ALL LIVES (SHOULD) MATTER, yet with new evidence daily, we are reminder of a truth contrary to this Ideal.

TRUTH: (n) that which is true or in accordance with fact or reality.

MEDICINE: (n) the science or practice of the diagnosis, treatment, and prevention of disease.

193

My Uncle Clarence Fowler, a genuine man that I admired tremendously, once stated that in order for Medicine to reach its maximum potency, the medicine and life, you will have to follow the instructions on its container, that being to SHAKE WELL. The most important compound within the vessel and medication of TRUE, is that of the TRUTH. It would seem that far too many have allowed their TRUE MEDICATION to reach its expiration date or have never had their prescriptions filled.

Let's explore the value of the TRUTH LAXATIVE. TRUTH, like the everyday Laxative, can't become functional if disregarded or left upon a shelf. Truth and the Laxative can't begin to work if it is not ingested and given proper time to produce MOVEMENT! When either moves, things have a tendency to flow, at first abruptly, and then when properly applied, smoothly. Once regular movement has been established, to maintain proper operation, one must have plenty of ruffage in their diet, i.e., dialogue, resolution, progressive positive ideas etc., of which the Fiber of True will be of daily routine. Benjamin Franklin once said, "Believe none of what you hear, and only half of what you see"! Both can be either, a half lie, or a half truth. So, if as the Bible states, Truth cometh by Hearing, and Hearing by

194

the Word of God, we must establish real Truth through in and of God!

My prescription for the ills and fallacies that have been a daily part of this nation, that has prompted the LIFE MATTERS movements can be found in the Word of God in the book of Matthew 22: 36-40.

Matthew 22: 36-40

36. Master, which is the Great Commandment in the Law. 37. Jesus said unto him, thou shall love the Lord thy God with all thy heart, and with all thy soul, and with all thy mind 38. This is the first, and Great Commandment 39. And the second is like unto it, thou shalt Love thy neighbor as thyself 40. On these two commandments hand all the law and the Prophets.

In the case of #ALL LIVES MATTER, let us examine a few of the tendencies which have led to the sorrow, vexation, and in some hearts the empathy that led to the #BLACK LIVES MATTER MOVEMENT, which should have been inclusive in the #BLUE LIVES, and #ALL LIVES MATTER AGENDAS, yet through far too many incidents, certain movements have been shown to have its fallacies, and are therefore exclusive.

Before I go any further in this chapter, allow me to reiterate, that I being a Child of God, hold true to the fact AND belief that truly #ALL LIVES MATTER in the Commandment to Love, and that #BLUE LIVE MATTER, with the exclusion of those of that are proven to be corrupt. When the proper protocol is evident in those sworn to protect and serve is applied, I am the first to commend, applaud, and pray for the protection and safety of those classified as BLUE. In view of the TROUBLES that are plaguing this nearly every segment of society, it is with sorrow and vexation of the heart that I conclude this book with an observation of the #ALL LIVES MATTER, #BLUE LIVES MATTER, and the #BLACK LIVES MATTER agendas that I pray will not just be a passing fad. Had #ALL LIVES MATTER, been a true concept, there would exist EQUAL EXPOSURE, EQUAL EDUCATION, and above all EQUAL OPPORTUNITY. Would it be plausible to expect a Criminal Justice System that isn't CRIMINAL?

Could it be that the Pharaoh's perceive that quite possibly the #BLACK LIVES MATTER, is a modern-day Moses screaming, LET MY PEOPLE GO? Pharaoh again would rather face the Red Sea, than to invite the slaves to the table of Education, Exposure, and Opportunity. Pharaoh would rather build a WALL, insuring that it would MAKE AMERICA GREAT AGAIN, than to erect a Bridge that spans the Abyss of hatred and inequality. Yes #ALLLIVESMATTER will be oh so welcomed when #ALLLIVES (TRULY) MATTER!

Had ALL LIVES MATTER, been of historical and factual validity the mantras of #BLUELIVESMATTER and #BLACKLIVESMATTER would be a non-factor that felt the need to be singled out to draw emphasis. If ALL LIVES MATTER, Universal Health Care would be a reality rather than a debated concept.

If ALL LIVES MATTER, why are there more funds allocated for Incarceration than of Education. Our nations prisons would not be proportionately more populated by Black and Brown inmates as its main proprietors and largest stockholders, and profiteers are white owned corporations. If ALL LIVES MATTER, there would be no differences in what is stated in the agenda of BLACK LIVES MATTER, and the 1776 Proclamation of Life, Liberty, and the Pursuit of Happiness that was intended for all. If ALL LIVES MATTER, some would not still be imprisoned with lengthy sentences for possession and distribution of a once controlled substance,

197

that some are now legally profiting from. There would be no difference for one who could afford an AFFLUENZA defense for the crime of Murder, and that of the IMTOOPOORENZA Defendant accused of the same crime. If ALL LIVES MATTER, then when some have been empowered and enriched through the blood, sweat, and tears of an entire race of people, and now the same race of people are being executed, disproportionately, at an alarming rate by some PEACE OFFICERS(NOT ALL), that are sworn to Protect and Serve! Why can't ALL see and realize, that we as a nation have an alarming problem that begs to emphasis #BLACKLIVESMATTER, NOW!

If ALL LIVES MATTER, the Truths we hold self-evident, would be evident for ALL and not to the exclusion of some. Had #ALLLIVESMATTER(ed), through the escalating actions, actions of many not been proven to be proven to be an untruth, the necessity of #BLACKLIVESMATTER, would be proven to be likewise. What does it profit us as a people, as a nation to possess the power to clear a forest, and move mountains, if there remains Stumps on the Plain that remains?

It's not a Republican or Democrat thing, it's not a Black or White thing, it is a Morality, versus Immorality thing. A thing that distinguishes between Wrong and Right!

There can be found Meekness in the Lamb that Roared:

Genesis 50:20-As for you, you meant evil against me, but God meant it for good, in order to bring it about as it is this day, to save many people alive.

Psalms 75:6-7-For promotion cometh neither from the east, nor the west, nor from the south, but God is the judge, he putteth down one, and setteth up another

Romans 8:28-And we know that all things work together for good to them that love God, to the who are called according to his purpose.

Psalms 127:1-Except the Lord build the house, they labour in vain that build it: except the Lord keep the city, the watchman waketh but in vain

The Tea Party meant to dissimilate hatred for the President of the United States, that actually motivated him to be more focused on legislation and truth to better the world, which in return garnered him the admiration of the world. Let us all be willing to put away our AT LEAST, to eventually attain the abundance of the MOST that God has in store for us all.

WELFARE would not be an issue if ALL were afforded equal quality EDUCATION, EXPOSURE, and OPPORTUNITY! Had #ALLLIVESMATTER, been of truthful essence, (R)Rep. Farnsworth of Illinois would not have stated, March 13, 1871, "The reason for the adoption (of the 14th Amendment)...was because of discriminating...legislation of those states...by which they were punishing one class of men under different laws from another class. (R) Rep. J.C. Watts stated on February 5, 1997, "We must be a people who dare, dare to take responsibility for our hatred and fears and ask God to heal us from within. And we must be a people of prayer, a people who pray as if the strength of our nation depended on it, because it does".

We are to "Shock this Nation with the Power of Mercy, for we are the Defibrillators of this Nation's Heart" a statement made during an address at the DEMOCRATIC NATIONAL CONVENTION of 2016 by Rev. William Barber that rings crystal clear in our collective consciences, to realize that their exists, legitimate discontent within #BLACK LIVES MATTER, and how can we embrace as a nation our deepest moral values if we heed not the cry! There should be evidence of your Proclamation of LIFE, LIBERTY, AND THE PURSUIT OF HAPPINESS through your actions. If you are who you proclaim to be, in the vernacular of the youth of this nation, "Don't just talk about it, #ALL LIVES MATTER, be about it!

To the proponents and boasters that hang their hats on the phrase "AT LEAST I'M", I can imagine it ruffled your feathers when the nation, and many parts of the world were enlightened during the DNC Convention with the statement of Jesus being a "Brown Skinned, Palestinian, Jew"! Imagine the audacity, the gumption! I can imagine some shouting "Tell 'um it ain't so Jesus"! I can laughingly imagine Jesus answering in his Jack Nicholson voice, "You want the truth, come on man, you can't handle the Truth'! After all what good can come out of Jerusalem, or the inner city"!

"ALL TRUTHS ARE EASY TO UNDERSTAND ONCE THEY ARE DISCOVERED, THE POINT IS TO DISCOVER!" - Galileo

#BLACKLIVESMATTER to the EXCLUSION of some, and to the INCLUSION of #ALL LIVES MATTER, is all we are saying! TRUTH!

Murder Unpunished

Oh, Oh, it's the PoPo! A recent analysis of Federal data on fatal police shootings by Investigative Non-Profit, Pro-Publica showed that young black males were twenty-one times more likely than their white peers of being shot and killed by police. The analysis conducted over a study of more than 12,000 accounts of police homicides from the FBI's supplementary Homicide Report during 1980-2012, focused in on the 1217 fatal shootings occurring between 2010-2012. An analysis of these homicides indicated that Black Teens between the ages of 15-19 were killed at a rate of 31.17 per million, and just 1.47 per million white males in the same age range were killed. Pro-Publica is an independent non-profit newsroom that produces investigative journalism, in the public interest. As quoted in Pro-Publica, "our work focuses exclusively on truly important stories, stories with moral force". We do this by producing journalism that shines a light on exploitation of the weak by the strong, and on the failures of those with power to vindicate the trust placed in them. Founded by Paul Steiger, the former managing editor of the Wall Street Journal Now led by Stephen Engelberg, former managing editor of the Oreonian, and former Investigative Editor of the New York Times and former assistant publisher of the Wall Street Journal, Richard Tafel

Police "Forces" are even more arrogant in carrying out their practice of law(less) enforcement. Possessing a menacing above the law persona, knowing the repercussions of their lawless duty could well lead to promotions as they are biasedly being investigated by their peers, as they enjoy paid vacations, i.e., Administrative Leave! How are we to teach our children to obey without fear and respect such law enforcement, when all they are bombarded with on a daily basis by the media are negative incidents and consequent results of incidents of overzealousness on the part of Bad Law Enforcement, undertrained, insensitive bullying by for a lack of a better term, legal, cowardly Terrorist! Again, I want to emphasize that not all Police Officers are BAD, yet there appears to be an alarming growing number within that realm.

It has become increasingly difficult to distinguish just who the Good Guys are. It has gone past the point of being distastefully disgusting, that after over fifty years ago when I questioned my Dad of the reasoning behind segregation, bigotry, and racism, my grandchildren are asking me the same DAMNED questions. It doesn't take a lot of strength to hang on, it takes a lot of strength to let go--J.C. Watts Choked out, "I can't breathe" in New York City, "Hands up don't shoot" in Ferguson Missouri, five shots to the back of a suspect being pursued by a Police Officer who is chasing said suspect as the officer "Feared for his life, as other Officers approached from the opposite direction in Muskogee Oklahoma, Brutalized and later found dead in her cell in Waller County Texas for the crime of improper use of a turn signal, and not showing proper respect to a DPS arresting officer, only a few instances of over aggressiveness by those sworn to protect and serve. Some may say, there exists a law of choice and consequences, yet, think for a moment, does that law apply equally in our Courts of Law, and public opinion, and in the minds of Rogue Cops? Of course, some will question why I have not brought up the scourge of Black On Black Crime, and I will question those who enquire, why hasn't the root causes of Black on Black crime been properly addressed and or attacked. The racial problems, and police problems in the nation are taking on an ugly, horrendous, us versus Them mentality, where victories on either side are few and shallow. The young men killed in previously mentioned incidents could well have been my son, your son, well truth be told, it could have been YOU!

How long will Lawless Law Officers, Lawless Lawyers, and Lawless courtrooms, and Lawless verdicts, be the rule, rather than the exception as it pertains to Liberty and Justice for ALL? Vengeance is mine saith the Lord. This that ye do to the least of these, ye do also unto me. Rest in Peace, those who have died needlessly and recklessly at the hands of supposed Peace Officers.

"Every unpunished MURDER takes away something from the serenity of every man's Life". - D. Webster.

SELECTIVE OUTRAGE

As a Teen in the early sixties, it was always curious to me as I was formulating opinions of life as a young Black Man, as to why there appeared to be a lack of empathy, and compassion from those opposite of me, and why there was little to no outrage as the result of daily news flashes, of those like me being attacked

205

viciously at lunch counters, those like me being beaten, clubbed, fire hosed, spat upon, and called everything but a child of God as those like me, who only wanted what was rightfully due citizens of the United States! Sometimes then as now, I wonder, where is the OUTRAGE(?)! Rogue Officers of the Peace then who chose to confront those like me with disdain, most certainly gave rise to the current wave of present-day Rogue Cops. Still, no outrage that would possibly bring about necessary, and long overdue change. Why the differences, as plain as Black and White?

Why does there exist one sports figure accused of sexual assault, allowed to pursue his hall of fame career, and charges subsequently swept under the rug of "Boys will be Boys", and another sports figure chose to protest hypocrisy and perceived wrongs in a peaceful manner yet is vilified? Yet I've always been taught that this is a democratic Nation, "Of the People, By the People, and For the People"! Why the misplaced and misapplied OUTRAGE? One's action in a sense glorified, and the other's action has led to his and let's be honest, Blackballing. Why has one's action led to more outrage than the others. Some will answer, "It's as simple as Black and White, and guess who makes the rules. Why is it we have always been and seemingly now more than ever, a nation who chooses to suppress rather than adequately addresses situations. We must AT LEAST, stop the practice of Majoring in the Minors, and Minoring in the Majors. Until you SEE Me, EXCUSE Me, as I do not share in your brand of enthusiasm, and Patriotism.

When our nation's current administration which incidentally ran on a slogan of "Make American Great Again" chooses to align itself with a Communist Regime, who incidentally not so long ago proudly boasted, "We Will Bury You", something is amiss when I fail to notice rightful OUTRAGE. When our Prisons for Profit, and Federal Prison Systems are bursting at the seams with those of a Brown or Black persuasion disproportionately, WHERE IS THE OUTRAGE? When a Professional Athlete exercises his constitutional right to take a knee in silent protest of unilateral wrongs, he perceives carried out contrary to what an Anthem and Constitution attempt to represent, oh now I see the outrage! He dared to silently and peacefully TALK BACK to the Grown(?) Folks. Shame on him, didn't he know the unwritten rule for second class citizens? That rule being, "You can be seen, yet don't seek to be heard"! It would appear his KNEE spoke

Volumes. How OUTRAGEOUS of him to not know his PLACE in a nation of Liberty and Justice for ALL!

Why pay dues of full membership when full benefits aren't applied to all members. Why pay full allegiance to a nation where some of its constituents by constitution were considered three fifths human? Why must the three fifths find it necessary to protest in any form to get one's attention to see eye to eye, and more importantly heart to heart? INTIMACY=In to me See!

Where is the outrage that when one holds up a mirror of moral integrity the one who is reflected that is offended find it necessary to objectify, vilify, nullify, and categorize the holder of said mirror. Yes, the United States is the Greatest Nation on earth, yet we must also admit, it is greater for some than it is for others. Where's the OUTRAGE? Why deny one's alienable right to call attention to a nation's great wrong, through a peaceful means as simple as taking a KNEE, a KNEE hopefully that has caused some to reassess some of their values, and reevaluate what PATRIOTISM really means in a God Fearing, divided United Nation. WHERE'S THE OUTRAGE(?)!!

Chapter 18

Closing Tidbits

COMPLACENCY-(n) A feeling of smug or uncritical satisfaction with oneself or achievements (syn) self-satisfaction

IGNORANCE-(n) lack of knowledge or information (syn) rude, unlearned, cluelessness.

"When that which is RIGHT is clearly WRONG, It's Hitting Too Close To HOME!

Close (adj) A short distance away or apart in space or time.

Welfare-(n) The Health, Happiness, and fortunes of a person or group.

Reciprocity-(n) The practice of exchanging things with others for mutual benefit, especially privileges granted by one country, or organization to another.

"This Nation in large part is guilty of haven chosen an easier wrong over (what should be) RIGHT!"

IGNORANCE

To be purposely ignorant of the pervasiveness within the notion of "ALL LIVES MATTER" displays deliberate ignorance of obvious factors that display the opposite. It would be truer statement to proclaim, ALL LIVES (SHOULD) MATTER. Yet some argue, and it pains me, even when some Blacks also question, "why don't Black Lives Matter to Blacks. My answer is the lack of Quality EDUCATION, Quality EXPOSURE, and Quality OPPORTUNITY, on both sides of the fence. Put the Man back together and the World will subsequently fall into place where ALL LIVES MATTER. One can't chop down tree of bigotry, hate and despair to clear the way to move mountains of negativity, only to leave stumps rooted in said bigotry, hate and despair. The Stumps must be along with their roots be eradicated.

Eradicate (v) - to remove (something) completely; to eliminate or destroy (something harmful).

The paradox of Wrong/Right being thought to be the Right for so long, that now Right/Right, seems wrong.

We can disagree and still love each other unless your disagreement is rooted in my oppression and denial of my humanity and right to exist.--James Baldwin

POST SCRIPT:

"If you can convince the lowest white man, he's better than the best colored man, he won't notice you're picking his pocket. Hell, give him somebody to look down on, and he'll empty his pocket for you!"—Lyndon Baines Johnson: What a real President was Like- Bill Moyer 11/13/88

"Most of us don't have a second chance to correct the mistakes of our youth. I do and I am."-LBJ

According to 1964 Census Bureau reports, lifetime earnings of an average black college graduate were lower than that of a white man with an eighth-grade education. LBJ to then leader of the Republican Senate, Everett Dirkson, "Shame, Shame, Shame!"

You cannot solve a problem from the same consciousness that created it. You must learn to see the world anew.–Albert Einstein

THE REPUBLIC FOR WHICH IT STANDS.

Pledge-(n) a solemn promise or understanding. (law) a thing that is given as security for the fulfillment of a contract or the payment of a debt and is liable to forfeiture in the event of failure.

Allegiance-(n) loyalty or commitment of a subordinate to a superior or of an individual to a group or cause.

Hypocrisy-(n) the practice of claiming to have moral standards or beliefs to which one's own behavior does not conform; pretense. (syn) dishonesty, deceit, mendacity.

Mendacity-(n) untruthfulness.

Patriotism-PATRIOTISM is emotional attachment to a nation which an individual recognizes as their homeland. This attachment, also known as national feeling or national pride, can be viewed in terms of different features relating to one's own nation, including ethnic, cultural, political or historical aspects. - Patriotism-Wikipedia, the free encyclopedia
(n) love that people feel for their country

212

Merriam-Webster Learner's Dictionary

Stand- (n) an attitude toward a particular issue; a position taken in an argument. (syn) attitude, stance, point of view, viewpoint, position.

PLEDGE of ALLEGIANCE

I Pledge Allegiance to the flag of the United States of America, and to the Republic for which it stands, one Nation under God, Indivisible, with Liberty and Justice for all.

Stands, Under God, Indivisible, Liberty, Justice, All. Please consider these words, sincerely when Pledging Allegiance. If it causes one to think, then consider its ramifications.

In conclusion, the statement made by LBJ about the "poor" white man and his feelings about the black man in 1964 was in the conscience of politics and social thinking then, and when the young white boy proudly proclaimed to me in 1970 when he felt justified and proud to proclaim to me, "At Least I'm White" as a badge of entitlement, as it is today in 2016. No Justice, No Peace! No Love, No Honor!

213

Within the greatest, independent nation on the planet earth, there remains so many different variations of separation, which is a kinder way of saying, this is the greatest nation on Earth where segregation is the rule, with very few exceptions. Let us examine the variant opposites that essentially need one another, to justify or even edify themselves, and their very existence. Just think what would writing be without reading, male without female, positive without negative, awake without asleep, plus without minus, loss without gain, wrong without right, night without day, life without death, democrat without republican, left wing without right wing, heaven without hell, angel without demon, liberal without conservative, dark without light, black without white, etc.. All things and everything have its opposite, yet without the opposites, where would assessment of values call home? How would one know of differences within social, economic, and political realms, where changes need to be applied, and where what works for all, definitely needs to be retained?

SEPARATION--a point, line, or means of division

SEGREGATION—the separation or isolation of a race, class, or ethnic group, by enforced or voluntary residence in a restricted area.

DEMARCATION–bound, circumscribe, define, delimit, limit

Keeping Love New--The Photo and the Rose, must the photo begin to fade, must the petals of the rose begin to wilt, before the vibrancy of the colors of life, the softness of the tender touch and feel of the petals, its pleasant fragrance fade before its value appreciated? Must the possibility of ABSENCE, be utilized, to awaken the sensation of PRESENCE? Must this nation perpetually be a Nation of Promise, and Potential, and permanently for some the Nation of could of, would of, and should of?

Love--(1 Cor. 13)--If this nation could truly begin to truly LOVE all of its citizens, in spite of our differences and not treat some as, "Johnny, who I can use, come lately", what have you done for me lately, sugardaddys, whores, pimps and poop on the lawn of

215

the elitist society, we will be able to really live the true meaning of "e pluribus unum", out of many, one.

A FEW GOOD MEN, FEW is the problem, where there should exist MANY. The Negro has a nature of survival, "Living on, and remembering the lessons of the SCRAPS thrown from the Master's table, whether it be from the Table of Exclusion, or the Table of Legislation. Is Power really meant to be used as a means of domination, to undermine, to be used as a divisive tool, to rule over and be blind to circumstances that have everything to do with the edification of said POWER? One segment of Society within the U.S. sincerely apologized to and given restitution, as another segment grudgedly apologized to, and essentially told to get over the wrongs done to an entire race of people, by a justified United Nation. It matters not the shade of -ism one applies to a pig, the rouge somehow never seems to completely cover all that is ugly, where there is an absence of Love! Whether those -isms be Nationalism, Socialism, Separatism, Conservatism, Liberalism, Capitalism, and/or RACISM.

A common man's simple observation of a complex issue, with a simple solution with the purest, and most glorious of intentions. Be very wary of becoming the

216

Empty Earthly Big Shot, while simultaneously being of no earthly good.

It would be easier for a camel to go through the eye of a needle, than for a rich man to enter into the kingdom of Heaven--Mark 10:25

What does it profit a man to gain the world, and lose his soul—Matt. 16:26

This is a book that is pleading with this nation to cancel its bill of sale for our souls. Over this book, I have pondered, rejoiced, agonized, procrastinated, been invigorated, promoted, and denounced. I had sometimes come to the conclusion of what is the use. Why had the need to write this book become a thorn in my flesh, needling my thoughts and spirit daily? If not now, when? For as Gandhi stated, "Health discontent is the prelude to progress". Thank you Dr. Wayne Dyer for helping me come to the realization that this undertaking, is something that I must do, something I have done, and not something that I will do, to state that I will do, infers that I haven't done, and it's not that I am going to be published Author, I AM a published Author.

217

Though some say the Negro overplays and overuses the "Race" card. I beg to differ! The actual card the Negro lives daily is more in the "Reality" genre. The Racial situations are very real, yet you don't relate for a lack of similar life experiences. I, and others like me are tiring of the Mediocre, mediocre souls, spirits, minds, love, treatment, nation, government and family experiences.

Thank you, former University of Texas Women's Track, and Life Coach Extraordinaire, Beverly Kearney for the revelation and admonition, that, NOW is the time of all aspirations and intentions, and thank you Dr. Wayne Dyer for the insight of what is NOW REAL. What I do NOW, may not rectify what was yesterday, yet it may justify what is to be. Thank you, Father, for the assignment, thank you for the opportunity to in a small way assist in being a salve for the healing of a nation. How can we, how will we ever, "Come Together", when we can't come together on coming together? A requirement for Birthing is PAIN, and the best medicine will have a nasty, bitter taste, that has to be shaken well to be of full effect.

Though the vision tarries (Hab. .2:3) We shall reap, if we faint not(Gal. 6:9) Old men will dream, Young men will have visions (Acts. 2:17)

EGYPT–E-EVIL, ENVIOUS, G–GREEDY, GLUTTONY, Y–YIELDING, P-PITIFUL, T-TORMENT, AND TRAVESTY! Don't go back down into EGYPT, come up out of EGYPT!

The ALIW., has a direct correlation to and with the ancient EGYPT, AT LEAST I'M PHARAOH'! Just as Pharaoh decreed, I'm getting my slaves back, certain factions of this nation's people, and political factions have decreed, we are taking our country back! My question to them is, back to what? Why go back down into EGYPT, when it appears that you are coming up out of EGYPT? Escape the Pharaoh syndrome! Thank you, Bishop T.D. Jakes, for helping me come to the realization, that I must come to a day of reckoning, to establish within my spirit, what my true worth, and happiness is. It is somewhat comical how the HAVES, the elite if you will, parallel the tendencies, and thinking of hate of ancient Pharaoh's. Although their rivers had turned to blood, and their lands were suffering plagues, it really didn't matter to them, just as long as they were still, to their thinking(in charge)

219

considered the ruling party, and they had their "At Least I'm Pharaoh" aura, and to hell with the rest of Egypt. Pharaoh was akin to the present-day so-called intellectuals of the radio talk show fame, that on more than one occasion, "RUSH" to their conclusions and judgements. I prefer to call them Egolectuals rather than intellectuals, who need and feed off those they perceive to be beneath them on any strata, and love those who unthinkingly agree with their message of fear, that is tryingly yet unsuccessfully masked hate, and arrogant entitlement, can anyone say "O'REALLY! Damn that Moses and his stick, damn that Obama and his schtick!

Just as it was with the pharaohs of the ancients, so it is today with the elites, both having the means of preventative measures to insure that their respective nations not perish, yet are unwilling to do what is necessary, only until such traumas affect them in a personal way, mainly because of their perceived "at least" pride, ego, and lack of love of mankind that is not of their kind, and love of one's self! Even when the right thing is being done, pride steps in, because of a sense of demotion, you are no longer in charge, and it is shown that you aren't a good follower, because you were given the cart, yet placed it before the horse, having never followed, you can't truly be qualified to lead, and you are not willing to admit such! Having not learned from the lessons of the past, we are assuredly doomed to repeat its tragic mistakes. Can you for one moment imagine what it is to be the Tolerated, Intolerable? Only tolerated when it is of benefit to you, either within the entertainment venues, or as being perceived to be of economic value. It must be awesome to control the red light, and the green light, while paying very small attention to the yellow caution light. Even if you have your AT LEAST, I can't be overly consumed with that aspect, I must be more absorbed by the prospect of my AT MOST.

"If you want to make the world a better place, take a look at yourself, and make that change--Man in the Mirror-Michael Jackson

Before that young man headed back down court after being beaten by at least twenty points, he angrily, and pointedly proclaimed to me, "At Least I'm White", a statement that at the time amused me, as I was thinking, what does that have to do with this basketball game. I came to the realization quite quickly that he was not referring to the basketball game, but rather his

221

perceived superior status in life. A standout Baseball pitcher caught cheating yet is still glorified, "At Least I'm White", O.J. Simpson, at least he thought he was white for a while, or at least he had white money, trumpeter of segregation now, segregation always, Gov. George Wallace, "At Least I'm White", the website "Save White People. com", At Least its White, the good, and lesser qualified graduate, who gets the job over the greater qualified candidate, more times than not it was because "At Least I'm White"! Face it, without Affirmative Action, Equal Employment, and various Civil Rights agendas some qualified Black candidates for jobs would not have been hired or even considered. It's not from the goodness of your heart, or that you truly were inspired to hire blacks, you were directed to through government mandates. Believe me, I am not of the opinion that all "AT LEAST" are detrimental. I am simply addressing those that are of a negative connotation, wherever and whenever they span culturally, from the most affluent, to the poorest.

Thank you, Bishop T.D. Jakes, for reminding me of the fact that "Excellence requires Discomfort". Sometimes life feels like an isometric exercise of the moral, and spiritual fibers within. I am either pushing or pulling, and that appears to be of little or no benefit, an exercise in

222

futility. Just keep on pushing and pulling, for it has been proven to be oh so true, "no pain, no gain"! The breaking is necessary for the building. When I settle for my AT LEAST-the least will be accomplished, contrary to my AT MOST-where I can and will do all things through Christ who strengthens me.(Phil 4:13). Come on nation, though the ship is being tossed, the skies are dark and ominous, and the shores of harmony seem afar, we must continue to row in unison toward the most we can be, and distance ourselves from the LEAST we are.

To have written this book, I knew that I would have nay-sayers, I would be questioned, and I would have haters. I would have internal, and spiritual debates, yet, nevertheless, this was something that purpose demanded of me, relentlessly. No matter how mundane, needless, worthless and or controversial anyone may feel this undertaking may be. You are welcome to cease reading and believe me I understand this will happen. If this happened to you, please examine what provoked your action, is it guilt, an unwillingness to examine one's self, or the arrogancy to feel, At Least I'm Me, and no one is qualified more than myself to hold up a mirror to my real self, the real me? Could it be the image you saw isn't the image you profess to be? US, the U.S., need to collectively examine US, bridge the divides, and crown thy good with brotherhood, from sea, to shining seas.

"Each one has to find peace from within. And peace to be real must be unaffected by outside circumstances".- M. Gandhi

God has truly shed His Grace on Thee, yet He can't be happy with what we are giving in return. Are we as a nation really walking, talking, and above all Loving as prescribed in His Holy Word? In the process, I imagine some Favor has been lost or delayed. Why does the hate, the bigotry, and negativity diminish at an excruciatingly slower pace, than that of a pre-global warming glacial iceberg?

So easily, the elite can laugh at the underlings, the butts of the jokes of society. To gaze into the mirror of truth, often leaves the gazee speechless. The elite weren't complaining when Chris Rock did a skit on the differences between Niggers and Negroes which was done using true life experiences, yet when Chris made comments on Slaves and Slavery, and Independence Day Celebrations, which also are true life experiences, he was challenged on his Loyalty and Patriotism for this Nation. Were you challenged when you gazed into the mirror, and not appreciate what was seen?

Why are those people constantly whining, why can't they be satisfied with the Scab? The cancer is still festering beneath the scab, waiting for its injection of true everlasting, effervescing, healing. Why is it this nation can think outside the box when it comes to technology, when it comes to intergalactic exploration, yet remain so within the box when it comes to situations here on earth concerning fair human interaction, the box of "Crowned Good, of Brotherhood" from sea to shining sea? We have the means and the capabilities of assuring that the DREAM becomes a reality for all mankind, the only deterrent being that of the closed mind, closed heart, and closed fist, as opposed to that of the open mind, open heart, and open hand of compassion. A change is gonna come! A change must come!

"In the course of history there comes a time when humanity is called to shift to a new level of consciousness, to reach a higher ground of morality. A time when we must shed our fears and give hope to one another. That time is now!"–Wangari Maathas, Nobel Prize winning founder of the Green Belt Movement (Kenya)

225

Fear causes one to stay at the Height, rather than plunge into the deep. How dizzying the heights attained when forced to look down. Is it truly fear, or is it selfishness? Pride is corrupted by arrogance. It would seem that some are saying, it is my heights that I have attained, and how dare one to feel that I should share such heights. Let them eat cake, let them eat cake.

SEPARATION the main component of degradation, COOPERATION the key component of elevation!

LOVE IS THE ANSWER, LOVE IS THE CURE!

I'm praying the EFFECT, of this book's AFFECT, to be that of the INFECT of Logic through Love!

1 John 3: 16-18 (NIV)

This is how we know what Love is. Jesus laid down his life for us. And that we ought to lay down our lives for our brothers and sisters. If anyone has material possessions and sees a brother or sister in need but has no pity on them, how can the Love of God be in that person. Dear Children, let us not love with words or speech, but with actions and in truth.

MADE YOU LAUGH

"Get White Church and Let's go Home"

Can't you just imagine Mr. Bubba, at his passing and approach to the Pearly Gates! Hell fire, Dat Gummit, Darn Dammit, it just ain't right, and they just ain't qualified!! This tirade occurring just as Mr. Bubba, places a pinch between his cheek and gums, adjacent to his porcelain veneers, and then spits out his chaw of Tobacco as he sips his complimentary Dom Perion, while dapperly dressed in starched overalls that protect his Giorgio Armani suit that is complimented by his Patent Leather Clod Busters.

As he strolls up to Heaven's Gate with his best egotistical, arrogant, entitled inquisition on the order of his AT LEAST world. He blurts out to Saint Peter, "I'll talk to you, because God is obviously too busy to talk to us HIS Chosen people these days"! I want to know somethin', How in the Hell, pardon my parley you franse '(French), How in the Hell can a White God, I know he's White, I've seen the pictures, of a White Nation, that been that way since its inception, with a White Constitution, Ben and Thomas them guys who writ it, allow a Fella (I ain't calling him a man yet) that ain't white, live in a White House, and be the most

Powerful Fella (I still ain't calling him a man) in all of God's White Creation!!??! Talk to me Pete, I'm listening, I'm waiting! I'll tell you what and I know it's true, it just ain't right I tell ya! By the way, pardon my AK47, Heaven is an Open Carry Kingdom, Ain't it?

We shall overcome, we shall overcome, we shall overcome someday, by any means necessary! I just come up with that un, you like it! Wait just a dad gum minute, I recollect I've heard that there phrase somewhere before. But It's catchy! Now can you kindly direct me to the White District of Heaven! Praise God!! He's last seen strolling along the Golden Streets singing his favorite hymn, "None but the Whiteous, none but the Whiteous, shall see God!

Just a little Church Humor which is incidentally the most segregated 3 hours in the United States Society. Flash forward a few years, and it appears that a Woman is the front runner to replace that Black Fella currently occupying the White House! You've got to know Bubba ain't taking that news too kindly, BUT he can take satisfaction in the fact that AT LEAST SHE'S WHITE!!! By the way Pete, you ain't no Muslim, are you?!!?

BIBLIOGRAPHY

Chapter 1 - Nobody Told Me, In the Beginning
1, 3, 4 - Brainy Quotes, M. Gandhi, Brainy Quotes.com
2 - Reference to a Television Commercial for Miller High Life Beer
5 - Rm. 8:28-KJV BIBLE

Chapter 2 - Mission Control
1, 2 - Definitions, Webster's Dictionary
3-6 - Biblical References, KJV BIBLE

Chapter 3 - It Was Good That I Was Afflicted
1, 2 - Biblical References, KJV BIBLE
3 - Lyrics from WHAT'S GOING ON, Marvin Gaye, 1971, Motown Records
4 - Definition, Dictionary.com
5 - Good Cop, Bad Cop Thesis, December 7, 2014, Parrish Miller.com

Chapter 4 - Lust of The Flesh, Lust of The Eye, Pride of Life
1,2 - Biblical References, KJV BIBLE
3-8 - Definitions-Dictionary.com

9-13 - Biblical References, KJV BIBLE
14-16 - MLK QUOTATIONS, Ripples Hope, Great American Civil Rights Speeches; Basic Civitas Books, 2003

Chapter 5 - Procrastination, Turn, Effort
1-4 - Definitions-Dictionary.com
5 - Eccl. 3: 1-8 KJV BIBLE
6 - Matt. 5:6 NLT BIBLE
7 - Matt. 22: 37-39 NLT BIBLE
8 - Prov. 23:7-KJV BIBLE
9 - Dan 5: 23-28 KJV BIBLE
10 - Definition-Dictionary.com
11 - Heb. 12:9 KJV BIBLE
12 - Quote, James Baldwin(1924-1987), BrainyQuotes.com
13-14 - Definitions, Dictionary.com

Chapter 6 - At Least Less Than Almighty
1 - Matt. 6:33 KJV BIBLE
2 - Mark KJV BIBLE
3 - Hosea KJV BIBLE
4 - 1 Peter. 2:.9 KJV BIBLE
5 - Phil. 4:13 KJV BIBLE
6 - 19 Biblical References, KJV BIBLE

Chapter 7 - Exclusivity and Entitlement
1 - John KJV BIBLE

Chapter 8 - Can't Buy Me Love
1.-2 - Definitions, Dictionary.com
3 – John KJV BIBLE
4 - 2 Chron. 7:14 KJV BIBLE
5 - Rm. 12:3 KJV BIBLE
6 – Ps. 23 KJV BIBLE
7 – I Cor. 10:13 KJV BIBLE
8 - 2 Tim. KJV BIBLE
9 – Ps. 30:5 KJV BIBLE
10 - Rm. 8:28 KJV BIBLE
11 - Luke 12:48 KJV BIBLE
12 - Isa. 64:6 KJV BIBLE
13 - Mark: 5: 28-30

Chapter 9 - Cycle of Enhancement, Deliver Us from Negativity
1 - 1 Cor. 3:16 KJV BIBLE
2 - Luke 9:23 KJV BIBLE
3 - Prov. 13:22 KJV BIBLE
4 - Has. KJV BIBLE
5 - Ps. 21 KJV BIBLE
6 - Quotation, Aristotle, Brainyquotes.com

7 - Quotation, Aristotle, Brainyquotes.com
8 - Rm. 12:19 KJV BIBLE
9-12 - Definitions, Dictionary.com
13 - Prov. 23•.7 KJV BIBLE
14 - Matt. 13:30 KJV BIBLE

Chapter 10 - After the Verdicts, Alchemies
1-2 - Definitions, Dictionary.com
3 - Nos. KJV BIBLE
4.- 6 - Definitions, Dictionary.com
7 - Rm. 13: 12-14 KJV BIBLE
8 - Matt, 20:16 KJV BIBLE
9 - Heb. 12: 1-3 KJV BIBLE
10 - Gal. 6:9
11 - Definition, Dictionary.com

Chapter 11 - Forgive Me, Cracked Bell
1.-6 - Definitions, Dictionary.com
7 - Rm. 4: 13-15 KJV BIBLE
8 - Quotation, Confucius, Brainyquotes.com
9 - Quotation, T.D. JAKES, TDJ.org
10 - Quotation, Voltaire, Brainyquotes@com
11 - Prov. 14:12 KJV BIBLE
12 - 2 Chron. 7:14 KJV BIBLE
13 - Jer. 18: KJV BIBLE

14, Matt. 25140 KJV BIBLE
15 - Matt. 25:45 KJV BIBLE

Chapter 12 - Thugs Ride
1 - Matt. 7: 1-3 KJV BIBLE
2 - Lyrics, Imagine, John Lennon

Chapter 13 - Prayerful Insight, Slanted Media
1 - Phil 4:13 KJV BIBLE
2 - Eccl. 9:11 KJV BIBLE
3 - Quotation, Edmund Burke (1729-1797) Brainyquotes.com
4 - Quotation, Confucius, Brainyquotes.com
5 - Quotation, Voltaire, Brainyquotes.com

Chapter 14 - How Long, Unworthy
1 - Isa. 40:31 KJV BIBLE
2 - 2 Thes. 31: 1-3 KJV BIBLE
3 - Gal. KJV BIBLE
4 - Ps. 30:5 KJV BIBLE
5 - 2 Chron. 7:14 KJV BIBLE
6 - Hos. KJV BIBLE
7 - Ps. 37:23 KJV BIBLE
8 - 2 Tim. 2:15 KJV BIBLE
9 - Quotation, Bishop D. Tutu, Brainyquotes.com
10 - Matt. 7:   KJV BIBLE

11 - Prov 23:7 KJV BIBLE
12 - Phil. 4:11 KJV BIBLE
13 - 2 Tim. 2:22 KJV BIBLE
14 - 1 Cor. 13:11 KJV BIBLE
15 - John. 13:34 KJV BIBLE
16 - Luke 11:17 KJV BIBLE
17 - 2 Cor. 6:14 KJV BIBLE
18 - John. 9:4 KJV BIBLE

Chapter 15 - Finish It, Hence, Therefore, Nevertheless
1 - Definition, Dictionary.com
2 - Inscription on the Statue of Liberty, Emma Lazarus
3 - 1 Cor. 13:2 NIV BIBLE
4 - 1 Cor. 13:2 KJV BIBLE
5 - Isa. 1:18 KJV BIBLE
6 - Ps. 133:1 NIV BIBLE
7.-9 - Definitions, Dictionary.com
10-17 - Definitions, Dictionary.com
18 - 1 Cor. 1:10 KJV BIBLE
19 - John. 13:34 KJV BIBLE

Chapter 16 – Pol (Tricks)
1 - Hos. KJV BIBLE
2 - Rom. 8:28 KJV BIBLE
3 - Prov. 16:25 KJV BIBLE

4 - Matt. 7:13 KJV BIBLE

5 - Quotation, Martin Luther, Brainyquotes.com

6 -10 - Bible Verses, KJV BIBLE

11 - Isa. 1:18 KJV BIBLE

12 - Prov. 16:32 KJV BIBLE

13 - Prov. 23:77 KJV BIBLE

14 - Luke 12:48 KJV BIBLE

15 - Rom. 12:3 NIV BIBLE

16 - Num. 22:23 KJV BIBLE

17 - Lyric, Ace, Van Morrison

18 – Hos. KJV BIBLE

19 - Quotation, H. Cain

20 - Luke 14:28 KJV BIBLE

Chapter 17 - The Necessary Outrage

1.-2 - Definitions Dictionary.com

3 - Matt. 22:36-40 KJV BIBLE

4 - 2 Chron. 14:7 KJV BIBLE

5 - Gen. 50.20 KJV BIBLE

6 - Ps. 75: KJV BIBLE

7 - Rms. 8:28 KJV BIBLE

8 - Ps. 127:1 KJV BIBLE

9 - Quote, (R) Rep. Farnsworth

10 - Quote, (R) Rep. J.C. Watts

11 - Quote, Galileo, Brainyquotes.com

12 - Article, Pro Publica

13 - Quote, J.C. Watts, Brainyquotes@com

14 - Quote, D. Webster, Brainyquotes.com

Chapter 18 - Closing Tidbits and Conclusion

1.-6 - Definitions, Dictionary.com

7 - Quote Brainyquote.com

8 - Excerpts, What a Real President was like, B. Moyer

9 - Quote, LBJ, Brainyquote.com

10 - Quote, A. Einstein, Brainyquote.com

11.-16 - Definitions, Dictionary.com

17.-19 - Definitions, Dictionary.com

20 - Mark. 10:25 KJV BIBLE

21 - Matt. 16:26 KJV BIBLE

22 - Hab. KJV BIBLE

23 - Acts 2:17 KJV BIBLE

24 - Quote, Wangari Maathai, Brainyquotes.com

25 - 1 John. 3:16

Made in the USA
Monee, IL
09 May 2022

96124757R00146